Time to Rebuild

Time to Rebuild

*A study in the book
of Nehemiah for today's
Church*

JOSEPHINE BAX

DARTON · LONGMAN + TODD

First published in 1996 by
Darton, Longman and Todd Ltd
1 Spencer Court
140–142 Wandsworth High Street
London SW18 4JJ

ISBN 0–232–52127–1

A catalogue record for this book is available from
the British Library

The Scripture quotations in this publication are taken from *The
New International Version* published and copyright 1973, 1978
and 1984 by International Bible Society.

The Alternative Service Book 1980
is copyright © the Central Board of Finance of the Church of
England. Extracts are reproduced by permission.
'Psalm 100' by Mary Calvert is quoted from *The Psalms: A New
Translation* by permission of A. P. Watt Ltd on behalf of The
Grail, England.

Phototypeset by Intype London Ltd
Printed and bound in Great Britain by
Redwood Books, Trowbridge, Wiltshire

PSALM 102

You, O Lord, sit enthroned for ever;
your renown endures through all generations.
You will arise and have compassion on Zion,
for it is time to show favour to her;
the appointed time has come.
For her stones are dear to your servants;
her very dust moves them to pity.
The nations will fear the name of the Lord,
all the kings of the earth will revere your glory.
For the Lord will rebuild Zion and appear in his
    glory.
He will respond to the prayer of the destitute;
he will not despise their plea.

Let this be written for a future generation,
that a people not yet created may praise the Lord.

(vv. 12–18)

Contents

Foreword

The Christian Church on earth is never more than one generation away from extinction. So it is hardly surprising that there is no shortage of people ready to prophesy its imminent demise! But, as the theologian Jürgen Moltmann once said, Christians are called to be 'purveyors of optimism'. It is in that spirit that Josephine Bax, with her customary freshness of style, provides a realistic counterbalance to prevalent cynicism and despair – by drawing together the ancient insights of the Book of Nehemiah and evidences of renewal within the contemporary Church of England.

At a time when this Decade of Evangelism has, mistakenly, been interpreted by some as a call to activism, it is helpful to be reminded, from the experience of Nehemiah's time, of the importance of prayerfulness and of the need for us to receive from God before we can in any way start to give. That is where the task of spiritual rebuilding which, undoubtedly, we face today must begin. Certainly in those places where the Church is alive and growing, the building up of Christ's body is undergirded by groups praying together and opening their hearts to the Holy Spirit that God may give the increase.

One of the unique aspects of Cross-winds, to which strong reference is made in this book, is that it mobilises Christians in a local area to come together to pray for the nation, for just one week in the year – and to become part of a process of prayer which, imaginatively, uses the national postcode grid. But, as the prophets of old and many generations of Christians, have discovered, spiritual renewal is invariably countered by opposition. Sometimes, however – and this is an important point made in this study – that opposition is of God. Discernment and assessment are as necessary in spiritual as they are in physical rebuilding. We can be fooled into thinking things are of the Holy Spirit when they are not at all.

Nehemiah is often studied alongside Ezra, since the two Old Testament books complement and explain each other. This study therefore looks at things from one particular angle. But Josephine Bax, whose writings in recent years about renewal have been widely valued, draws from the one source some wisely balanced points. Proper concerns for justice and peace must also allow room, among the faithful remnant, for the courage to have new visions – not least about corporate worship, repentance, commitment and celebration. And there is a healthy dose of realism too about the discipline and perseverance needed if our attempts at rebuilding are to bring lasting results.

At a time when the Old Testament stories are little known among the faithful – and smaller books like Nehemiah scarcely at all – this study is a useful reminder of the importance of recapturing the message of these ancient works, so familiar to Jesus and so sadly neglected in our day.

+NIGEL MCCULLOCH
Bishop's Lodge, Wakefield, December 1995

Introduction

This book is written out of a conviction that God is speaking to us through the book of Nehemiah today. My book is not a commentary in the accepted sense of that word, <u>rather it is a prophetic call to prayer and action</u>. It is written from a background of having worked in the Church of England for the past twenty years, and from my experience of that Church at every level, parish, deanery, diocesan and national.

The Church in England today is in crisis. It is being shaken and stirred, it is crumbling in some places and being rebuilt in others, it is in decline and renewal, it is experiencing death and new life. But crisis is what leads to renewal; the tottering walls have to be taken down before they can be rebuilt. This process has been going on piecemeal now for the past few decades, but the conviction behind this book is that now is God's time, *kairos*, now is the moment, for which God has been preparing us over a lifetime. He wants, I believe, to rebuild his Church and restore this nation, and he wants to do it now. It is God's work, but he needs our co-operation, our willingness to be part of his overarching plan, and I believe that he is showing us that plan through the wonderful book of Nehemiah.

A reminder that we look to the Scriptures against a certain context and to hear God's word for now.

I hope that *Time to Rebuild* will inspire you to reread the book of Nehemiah, or to read it thoroughly for the first time, and to tackle the questions at the end of each of my chapters, either on your own or in a group. I think you will find, as I have, something of the depths and richness of it, and its application to our present-day situation. It is amazingly topical, and as one person I talked to said, 'It rings bells, because that's how things are.'

I am very grateful to all those who have contributed to this book and helped me to write it. I wish to thank Barbara Steele-Perkins, the Revd Graham Earney, the Revd Patrick Revell, the Rt Revd David Pytches, John Bimson, Anna Tambling and Capt Phil Baines.

From the Bath and Wells Diocesan Renewal Group I would particularly like to thank the Revd Preb. John Simons, the Revd Preb. Patrick Riley, the Revd Adrian Hallett and the Revd Richard Salmon.

My grateful thanks to Pat Southway, who typed the manuscript, and to Mark Taylor who helped me to put it together. They have all added richness and rootedness to this present-day account and a breadth of experience to add to my own.

I pray that this book may be a source of encouragement to all who read it, and that it will help them to see more clearly the particular piece of the task of the rebuilding that God is calling them to. May he who is calling us to the task enable us to do it, for his name's sake. Amen.

JOSEPHINE BAX
September 1995

1

Prayer for the Nation

The book of Nehemiah opens with bad news. About the time that this book speaks of (445 BC) some of the Israelites (including Nehemiah) were still in exile in Babylonia, while others were struggling to restore Jerusalem and live there. Nehemiah receives the bad news that those trying to live in Jerusalem are in extreme difficulty. The walls of Jerusalem have been broken down, and its gates have been burned with fire. This means that the inhabitants have no defence against their enemies and are open to any form of attack.

Nehemiah responds to this news with mourning and fasting. He weeps for his people and prays for them. Judging by what follows he is not only identifying with the suffering of his people, but is identifying with the heart of God, which is also grieved. The intercessor identifies both with those for whom he or she is praying, and also with the heart and will of God in the situation. Nehemiah's prayer of intercession is recorded in this first chapter, and is of great interest, as it is a model of how to intercede.

First of all Nehemiah recalls who it is he is speaking to – the great God of heaven, whose nature is that of faithful love, who keeps his covenant with those who love him and obey his commands. It is essential in intercession to remember who it is we are speaking to – what a great God he is and his claims on us – and then we will not fall into the trap of simply handing God a shopping list of things we want him to do.

Florence Nightingale wrote in the margin of her diary, 'I must remember that God is not my personal private secretary!' It is good to start a time of intercession with worship – giving God his worth and praising him for who and what he is, not just because he deserves our worship, but because we need to remember whom we are approaching. So Nehemiah reveres God and does not tell God what to do. On behalf of his people he confesses the way in which they have disobeyed God and he includes himself and his family in this. Nehemiah is portrayed in this book as a righteous man, nevertheless he does not say, 'They have sinned', about his people, but 'We have sinned', identifying himself completely with those he is praying for.

Then he reminds God of his covenant with Moses, and of his promise that, if his people return to him and obey his commands, he will gather them together and bring them into the Promised Land which God has chosen 'as a dwelling for my Name' (1:9). The nature of intercession is that it asks God to do what he has intimated that he wants to do, or has promised to do. Intercession asks for what is on God's heart, whilst petition asks for what is on our heart. Nehemiah is simply praying that God will do his will in the situation, reminding him of what he has done in the past for the people of Israel, and of what he has shared with them of his purposes for

2

their nation. Nehemiah is thus able to ask what God has already intimated that he would do. For this reason he prays that God will hear his request, and give him success in persuading the king to allow him to return to Jerusalem and do something about the situation. His intercessory prayer opens doors in heaven that allow things to happen on earth, and the rest of the book of Nehemiah unfolds as the result of the prayer being answered.

The state of our nation today is also bad news. High unemployment, rising crime rates, family and community breakdown, drug addiction, and home-lessness make this an increasingly unhappy and divided country. The Church, which should have the answer to these problems, is itself in sharp decline, and Great Britain can no longer be called a Christian country. The Church, like most of the Israelites in the book of Nehemiah, finds itself as it were in exile in a secular society which nevertheless has its own pagan gods. Both Church and nation need rebuild-ing, spiritually and socially, if our nation is to come back to spiritual and moral health. It is a formidable task, but we need to start, where Nehemiah started, with intercessory prayer. With human beings the rebuilding of Church and nation is an impossible dream but with God all things are possible. We must start by coming to him in penitence and faith, asking him to intervene, to turn the tide, to rescue us from ourselves.

As with Jerusalem, where the walls had to be rebuilt first to make the city safe from her enemies before work could begin on the temple and the exiles could return to rebuild the nation, so with our situ-ation now. The walls of faith and confidence in God need to be rebuilt to protect our society, so that the Church and nation can recover from their sharp decline. As well as the walls of faith we need those with prophetic gifts to bring us warnings and encouragements about the rebuilding process. Many people in our society have a residual belief in God, but the walls of faith have been eroded by cynicism and unbelief, within the Church as well as outside it. Rebuilding confidence is the prime task if both the system of belief we call the Church, and also the life of the nation are to be rebuilt. In order to start the process we need a wave of prayer to go up to the heart of God in intercession so that the doors can be opened in heaven and on earth for this to happen.

Several prayer initiatives have come into being with this in mind. The Lydia group of women intercessors have been praying for many years for Britain, but in recent years they have been praying that other intercessors will join them. They have been asking God to give the clergy a real heart for intercession and also that the lay people will join them in the task. Their prayers are being answered in the prayer initiatives that have come into being in the last few years. The Quarterly Prayer Initiative was started by Bob Dunnett to pray for spiritual revival in this country. It calls intercessors to give a day once a quarter to pray for the nation. The Noon Prayer Initiative was launched by David Ward to encourage people to pray at noon every day for the nation. The Cross-winds Prayer Initiative was launched in 1994 to encourage churches to give a week a year to pray for the renewal of God's people, the rebuilding of his Church, and the restoration of the nation to

Christ. These prayer initiatives are overlapping rather than being in competition with each other. When they came together to meet and share the vision each had been given they found that God had been preparing them over a long period of time for this work, but all agreed that now is God's time, *kairos*: this is the moment when God has particularly chosen to act.

The idea for Cross-winds started in 1991, when John Simons, Rector of Holy Trinity, Nailsea, Bristol, was invited by Dr George Carey, then Bishop of Bath and Wells, to take a sabbatical and go to the Far East to study patterns of church growth in that part of the world. Spending some time in Korea at the church of Dr Yonggi Cho, which has grown at an astonishing rate over recent years, he was convinced that their commitment to prayer was the prime factor. Prompted by the prayer example of this and other churches in five other nations he visited in the Far East, together with a knowledge of past prayer movements in the British Isles, John came back convinced that something further needed to be done to mobilise prayer for Britain.

As a result of further thought and prayer, an initial pilot project was launched in Bristol, in collaboration with the Greater Bristol Ecumenical Council. This was followed by the launch of Cross-winds in the South-west at Wells Cathedral on 27 November 1993. The initiative was named Cross-winds to express the truth that God will honour that which reflects the finished work of his Son on the cross, and is done through the power of the wind of the Spirit. It is interdenominational, and uses the national postcode grid for distributing information and co-ordinating the participating churches.

In January 1994 all the churches throughout the South-west were contacted with the help of the Bristol Christian Resource Centre's comprehensive database. They were asked to give a week during 1994 and 1995 to praying for the Church and nation. Each church approached was asked to hold daily prayer events during their week for the church, their local town/village, their nearest city, their postcode area, and for the nation and its leaders. The response to this request has been so great as to ensure that until the end of 1995 a constant wave of intercessory prayer will go on throughout the South-west for the Church and the nation.

Before all this got under way, a trainee Non-Stipendiary Minister, who knew nothing about Cross-winds, or the plans being made for its launch, came up to John Simons after a service in his church and asked him to help explain a puzzling vision that he had had.

He had woken up in the middle of the night and had seen an outline of Britain as if he were looking down on it from a satellite. 'Watch and see what happens,' he was told.

A wind blew up. 'Where is the wind blowing from?' he was asked. He noticed that it was coming from the South-west. 'Watch and see what happens,' he was urged again. He noticed that there were white sparkling particles like snowflakes or petals blowing in the wind. As he watched, the particles settled right across the country in the shape of a cross, and the foot of the cross stood in the South-west. While he was wondering what this meant, the answer came, 'I have called my people in the South-west to come around the foot of the cross and pray, because I wish to call this nation back to myself.' The astonishment of the man at this vision was increased all the more when he heard about the Cross-winds initiative. Those of us involved in Cross-winds believed that this vision confirmed that the initiative was indeed the work of God's Holy Spirit and in tune with God's will.

It is interesting to notice that the logo for the Decade of Evangelism has been drawn at an angle so that if it is placed across a map of Britain, the foot of the cross is again in the South-west. The logo is drawn in this position, not upright as one would expect, so that coincidentally it confirms the vision that the Non-Stipendiary Minister had. (See diagram 1.)

Before I knew about Cross-winds God was calling a group of people including myself to the rebuilding of the Church. I had come back from the World Conference on Evangelism, Brighton '91, full of good ideas, things I had learnt at the excellent conference. I wrote down what I wanted to do and sent the prayer list to those who kindly pray for me and for my ministry. As soon as they started to pray I felt God saying to me, 'Ask me what I want.' So I said, 'Show me what you want and I will do it, there's no point in doing anything unless you want it.' He started to speak to a group of us in my parish and also in the Bath and Wells Renewal Group, through the book of Nehemiah about the rebuilding of the Church.

To me the words came quite distinctly, 'I want to rebuild my Church.' I shook, because that was what

Diagram 1

God had said to me when I was called into full-time Church work in 1969. The years in between had been a preparation, but now was God's time, *kairos*, the time for it all to happen.

The Diocesan Renewal Group decided to run a teaching programme on the book of Nehemiah entitled 'Time to Rebuild'. I was asked to lead the first session on chapter one. As I prepared my talk, I felt led to take Nehemiah's prayer, and turn it into a Christian prayer for what I believed that God had been showing us he wants: the renewal and rebuilding of the Church, and the restoration of the nation to Christ. The Church is at such a low ebb that only the Spirit of God acting in power can do this.

If it is what God wants, why do we have to pray for it? Why doesn't he just do it? As I understand it from the Bible, God looks for those who will intercede on behalf of the people. He looks for a channel through which to act. The prophet Isaiah says:

The Lord looked and was displeased that there was no justice. He saw that there was no-one, he was appalled that there was no-one to intervene [or intercede]; so his own arm worked salvation for him, and his own righteousness sustained him. (Isaiah 59:15b-16)

Ezekiel 22:30 says:

I looked for a man among them who would build up the wall and stand before me in the gap on behalf of the land so that I would not have to destroy it, but I found none.

The Lord is a God of justice, and we deserve his judgement, but he is also a God of mercy who longs to save us, even from the mess that we have made. If a righteous person, i.e. someone who is right with God, intercedes according to God's will, he will hear, and the doors in heaven will open so that his will is done on earth.

The righteous person listens to God, and hears what he has to say about the situation. It is my experience that if we draw aside to listen to God, he will speak to us, and show us what he wants to do. We then agree with God and his purpose, and pray as a response to what we believe that God is saying. We should pray according to the character of God as we know it from Scripture, as Nehemiah did, and try to see the situation as God sees it. It is also necessary, as we are 'standing in the gap' between him and his people, to identify with the person or people that we are praying for, and to love them. Like Abraham in Genesis 18 we need to display both humility and boldness in our approach to God, even more so now that we can approach God through Jesus Christ. In doing so we share in the priestly ministry of Jesus who is interceding for us (Hebrews 7:25). Because all the references to Jesus' intercession in the New Testament refer to him interceding for the Church and not for the world, a theory has grown up among intercessors that he is praying for the Church, and we should be praying for the world. This is a contentious issue, but what is certain is that we can approach God with boldness in intercession, because he has made a New Covenant with us through the merits of his Son Jesus Christ. 'Through Jesus Christ our Lord' is not just a deferential phrase but the key to doors in heaven being opened. To know how to pray we need to listen, to identify with both God's position and the position of those for whom we pray, and we need to rely on the Holy Spirit to show us how to pray according to the will of God. If we are led by the Spirit in prayer, and come to the Father through Jesus Christ our Lord, then we shall please God and obtain what we ask. Having asked we need to trust God for the outcome, we have prayed and we should look for the prayer to be answered. (See diagram 2.)

The prayer that I based on the intercession of Nehemiah (1:5–11) has been adopted as the Crosswinds prayer. It follows the intercessory pattern that I outlined above. It is based on the New Covenant that we have with God through his Son Jesus Christ. It asks for what I believe that God wants to do, i.e. to renew and restore his people, to rebuild his Church, and to win this nation for Christ and his gospel once again. By praying, by attempting to be in tune with the will of God, we ourselves are prepared for what God wants to happen. He can make us channels for what he wants to do, just as he made Nehemiah a channel through which he could work to achieve his purpose, the restoration of Jerusalem, so that the restoration of the nation of Israel, the rediscovery of the Scriptures and the rebuilding of the temple, could follow. Prayer is followed in the book of Nehemiah by action, but prayer comes first. So it must be with us. We need to be in tune with the will of God for his Church and for the nation, we need to intercede on their behalf, so that God can act in his sovereign way to save and help us.

At the time of writing Cross-winds is expanding

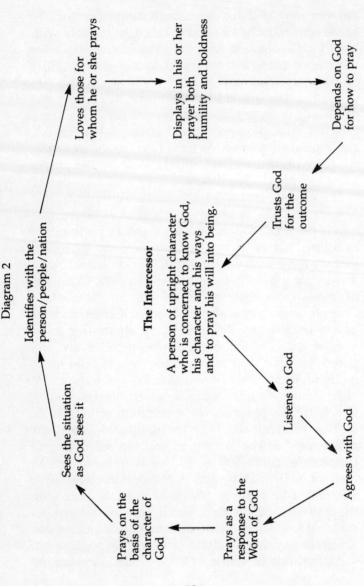

Diagram 2

Loves those for whom he or she prays

Displays in his or her prayer both humility and boldness

Depends on God for how to pray

Trusts God for the outcome

Identifies with the person/people/nation

The Intercessor

A person of upright character who is concerned to know God, his character and his ways and to pray his will into being.

Sees the situation as God sees it

Listens to God

Prays on the basis of the character of God

Agrees with God

Prays as a response to the Word of God

(From a diagram by Barbara Steele-Perkins)

12

to become a national, not just a South-western initiative. It was launched nationally (in partnership with Noon) at the House of Lords on 21 February 1994, at a meeting covened by Simon Reading. Most exciting of all, revival is breaking out in churches right across the country. There is some questioning as to whether this is the revival we have been praying for, or whether it is what the Bible calls a 'time of refreshing from the Lord' (Acts 3:19). Whatever you call it, there is an outpouring of the Holy Spirit going on. Already people are being converted, healed, stirred to repentance, encouraged, helped, challenged. If it is to continue to spread we need to go on praying that God will carry on pouring out his Spirit on the Church and nation today.

Cross-winds Prayer

Lord God of heaven, you are great, and we stand in awe of you. You faithfully keep your New Covenant with those people who trust in you, and Jesus Christ, whom you have sent. Look down on us, Lord, and hear our prayers, as we pray for your Church here in this nation. We confess that we, your people, have sinned. We and all the whole people of the nation have gone away from you and your gospel, the Good News about Jesus Christ.

Remember now what you have done in him, and not what we deserve. For his sake, renew and restore your people, rebuild your Church, and win this nation for Christ and his gospel once again.

We ask this in his name, and for your honour and glory. Amen.

Study

BIBLE READING: NEHEMIAH 1

QUESTIONS FOR MEDITATION/DISCUSSION

1. What does Nehemiah's prayer have to tell us about:
   (a) his relationship with God,
   (b) how to pray?
2. What is there about today's Church and society that you particularly think needs our prayers. (If in a group, make a list on a wallchart which you can refer to in your prayer at the end.)
3. What can you and your church do about it?

PRAYER

Pray for the Church and the nation using the list you have made for reference, and ending with the Cross-winds prayer.

For further information about Cross-winds, write to:

Cross-winds, 42 Friar Gate, Derby DE1 1DA.
Tel.: 01332 349409
Fax: 01332 200185.

2

Faith to Rebuild

In chapter 2 we have moved on four months from when Nehemiah first heard the bad news about Jerusalem. It is now the month of Nisan (March-April) in the twentieth year of King Artaxerxes' reign (445 BC). Four months of waiting, praying, and uncertainty have passed. So often when testimonies are given we are left with the impression, 'I prayed, and my prayer was answered straightaway'. In many cases, however, there is a time of waiting and uncertainty when we have to exercise faith in God for the situation we are praying for. The answer seems to come agonisingly slowly, and when it eventually comes, it is not always what we expected.

At last the opportunity comes for Nehemiah to speak to the king. In doing so he is putting his life on the line. It was not acceptable for the servants of the king to be sad in his presence; whatever their private feelings were, they were supposed to be cheerful in front of him. But Nehemiah shows his feelings, and sure enough, the king asks him what is the matter. Although he has been praying with fasting for four months, Nehemiah shoots what is called an 'arrow' prayer to God before he answers. He tells the king that the city where his ancestors

15

are buried is in ruins, and asks permission from the king to go and rebuild it. Nehemiah's prayers are resoundingly answered: not only is the king's permission given, but the king provides timber for the gates of the ruined city and an escort of cavalry to go with him. Armed with the necessary papers, Nehemiah travels to Jerusalem. It is not long before the first hint of trouble comes, with two men, Sanballat and Tobiah, making it clear that they are very disturbed at the arrival of someone to help the Israelites in Jerusalem. Sanballat is the governor of Samaria, and Tobiah the governor of Trans-Jordan. Their opposition is political rather than religious, their authority is threatened by Nehemiah's coming.

After staying in Jerusalem for three days, not telling anyone why he has come, Nehemiah rides out to inspect the damage that has been done to the walls of Jerusalem. The damage is indeed severe: in one place the piles of rubble prevent his mount from getting through. Having inspected the ruins, he then shares with the leaders in Jerusalem why he has come, and encourages them to join in the task of rebuilding the walls. Without the walls the city is vulnerable to attack from enemies, and there would be no point in rebuilding the city or the temple. The response is positive – 'Let us start rebuilding' – and they begin straightaway.

Right from the start there is opposition. Sanballat and Tobiah ridicule the whole endeavour, and accuse them of rebelling against the king, which is patently not true. Nehemiah answers them by saying that God will bless the Israelites' efforts at rebuilding, and give them success, but that the dissidents will have no share in Jerusalem or claim to it.

What has this to say to us today, and what relevance has it to the situation that we are in? I believe that what we need to do today is to rebuild the walls of faith, so that in their turn the Church and nation can be rebuilt. Without faith in God we are open to every kind of attack, and every kind of pressure in the modern world. Just as the walls of a church enclose the space in which the worship of God can be carried on, so the walls of faith enclose the space within which God's will can be done, his Kingdom come. Ever since before the First World War which shattered the secure Edwardian world in which people had been living, and eroded their faith in God, the Christian faith has been in decline, and now there remains only a tiny remnant who take their faith seriously.

The time has come to rebuild those walls of faith, on which the prophets will stand to warn and encourage the people of what is coming. At the moment all they have to stand on is a pile of rubbish, the remnants of what once was.

Self-confidence has taken the place of confidence in God. Modern man and woman feel more in control of their destiny, more in control of the forces of nature, more able to survive by their own efforts than previous generations. But the cracks in this self-confidence are beginning to show as society splits apart, crime rises, families break up, and racial tensions, wars and erosion of the environment gnaw away at the foundations on which our civilisation is built. Science and politics are no longer seen to have the answers to a better life.

Although only a tiny remnant now goes to church on Sundays, more than seventy per cent of people in this country say that they believe in God. But what kind of belief do they mean, and what kind of God? Even among churchgoers there is a decline in faith in the kind of God that we meet in the Bible. The God that speaks to us through the Old Testament and the New is a God who initiates relationships, who intervenes in human history and leaves his mark on it, who is ultimately in control – although human freedom and the devil's rebellion can cause disaster in the short run, in the long run God will have the last word. He is a God who reveals himself to us, who speaks to us, who desires that we should have a dynamic relationship with him. Above all, through Jesus Christ, he calls us to 'Follow me'. This is a call that cuts across our self-confidence and self-motivation. It is no accident that one of the best-selling pop records ever is Frank Sinatra's 'I did it my way'. What we need is a faith in God that will lead us to do it *his* way, not ours. Most humbling of all, in our relationship with God we cannot justify ourselves, though many down the ages have tried.

We can only rely on God's grace and mercy which is mediated to us through Jesus Christ. Many are willing to give, but how many are willing to receive what Jesus has done for us, and what the Holy Spirit wants to do in us now? How many even know what is on offer? That includes many churchgoers. It is assumed that anyone who goes along to church on a Sunday will just pick all this up, but this is not necessarily the case. A Diocesan Training Officer said to me, 'The trouble with this diocese is that people are under the Law (trying to justify themselves to God) rather than the gospel (which is about receiving what God has done for us!).' In spite of all the efforts that the churches make, an enormous job of communication still needs to be done to build faith in the God who is revealed to us in Scripture. Only with God's help, and in the power of the Holy Spirit, can it be done. Our churchgoers need evangelising, as well as those outside the Church. When they have really heard, understood and been obedient to the gospel, then our churches will be dynamically changed.

All we can see at the moment is the rubble of the walls of faith, and a tiny remnant who are clinging on in spite of the difficulties. Is there anything we can do to change the situation?

I believe that Nehemiah himself gives us the inspiration as to how to proceed. As we saw from the previous chapter, he starts with prayer, and as we see from this chapter he continues to pray throughout. Having first secured God's help through a sustained effort of prayer, he then approaches the worldly authority under which he is set, for permission to proceed with the work. Through the power of prayer he not only gets permission to proceed, but also the resources he needs.

We are all under authority, and I believe God means us to work in that way. If we approach the task prayerfully, and if we are in God's will, the way will be open for us to be able to work, and the resources will be made available to us for the task. It is essential to have the support of those in authority over us, and a prayerful approach will open doors to enable us to function. God never gives us a call without making available the means to answer it. If he is calling us to rebuild faith, he will make it possible for us to do this, though not necessarily in the way in which we envisage.

How do we build faith, for ourselves and for others? If you want to see how important faith is, just look up in a concordance to see how many references there are to faith in the New Testament: thirty-seven in the epistle to the Romans alone. Jesus tells us that all we require in order to move mountains is a tiny speck of faith as small as a mustard seed (Matthew 17:20). This tiny speck of faith is God's gift to us, we cannot work it up. However, it represents a confidence in the God shown to us by Jesus, so that we believe not only that he exists, but that he is the kind of God we can have confidence in. Having faith doesn't mean that we shall be without doubts or questions, but the questions that spring from faith are different from those prompted by unbelief. Unbelief can never discern the things of God, or come to the truth about how things really are; we need that tiny speck of faith to be given to us by God, and we also need the Holy Spirit of God, who will lead us into all truth (John 16:13). For without the Spirit we cannot understand or know the things of God or come to spiritual understanding. St Paul says, 'The man without the Spirit does not accept the things that come from the Spirit of God, for they are foolishness to him, and he cannot understand them, because they are spiritually discerned' (1 Corinthians 2:14). So we need to pray for the gift of faith, and the gift of the Spirit of God to lead us into all truth, for ourselves and for others. Then the crucial thing is to go out and live the life of faith, so that our faith will grow. When I first became a Christian, I can remember thinking, 'If all this is right, then it will work, the only way to find out is to live as if it is so.' Forty years later I am still living by faith, but my faith has grown in those years as I found God to be true, right, and faithful, though I have come through times of testing along the way.

So we need to have three things in order to build faith, for ourselves and for others – the grain of faith, the Holy Spirit and a willingness to be led by him, and the willingness to live out the life of faith. It seems disarmingly simple, yet the most difficult thing to do for many of us is to say that unequivocal 'yes' to God, not just once, but continuously throughout our lives. Many barriers stand in the way, among them sin and selfishness, but above all we experience fear, and an unwillingness to trust God. It is reassuring to read of the disciples being afraid; they too were frightened to death by what Jesus was doing, frightened of what people would say, frightened of the authorities. In spite of that they overcame their fear when the Holy Spirit came upon them; he gave them the courage to rise above their very natural anxieties and go out to live the life of faith and proclaim the gospel.

This is all the gift of God: the faith, the Holy Spirit, the grace to live out the life of faith; all we have to do is to receive, to say our 'yes' to what God wants to give us. He says to us as he said to those first disciples, 'Do not let your hearts be troubled and do not be afraid' (John 14:27). I see my job as Renewal Adviser as helping people to receive what God has to give them, sharing with them the confidence that I have learnt in order to help them say their 'yes' to God even through times of pain and difficulty.

This is the work of evangelism to new Christians,

the work of renewal to established Christians, and the work of rebuilding – rebuilding of faith, of the Church, and of society. We can only give to others what we have first received from God ourselves, so it is essential for us to receive and go on receiving from God all that we need to live the life of faith.

The trouble is that for most people their relationship to God is seen in terms of giving rather than receiving. We pray to God rather than listen and receive *from* him, we try and live our own lives according to our ideas of what that should be, rather than let ourselves be led by the Spirit of God. It is God who initiates, God who leads, God who gives; we need to learn to listen and receive, to trust and obey. This is what being a follower of Jesus means, not speaking to him in a monologue without letting him have a word in edgeways, not exhausting ourselves in endless good works, but receiving from God, and then giving to others what we have first received from him. To do this we need the grace of humility and obedience, to carry out God's will rather than doing 'our own thing', but most of all we need that trust in God, that confidence in him which we call faith.

He who calls us is himself faithful, deserving of our trust. One of the most common ways of describing God in the Old Testament is the Hebrew word *hesed* or 'constant love'. God's love is not fickle or easily changed. Unlike the other gods worshipped by the nations surrounding the Jewish people, who were temperamental, difficult to please, and whose response could not be relied on, the God of the Israelites was constant, faithful, loving, caring, merciful and all-powerful. He wanted the greater good of his people, and they could turn to him in confidence, in repentance if they had sinned, but knowing that they would get a right response from him, because he loved them.

This is God our creator, the God who made us, who numbers the hairs on our head, who knows us better than we know ourselves. Nehemiah turns to God in utter confidence, convinced that the God who cared for his ancestors cared for his people now, convinced that God was all-powerful and in control, convinced that though his people had sinned God was merciful and would forgive. Nehemiah's prayer of faith and confidence in the God whose character he knew was answered. The way was made possible for him to return to Jerusalem and rebuild, by the co-operation of the king, and above all the co-operation of the people of Jerusalem, who then immediately responded 'Let us rebuild' and started to get on with the work.

In our day God is already bringing together groups of people to share in this work of rebuilding. For I believe it is not going to be accomplished by particular leaders, but it will be achieved by small groups of people all over the country coming together to pray, share, study and work to build first their own faith and then the faith of others. Led by the Holy Spirit they will receive the grace and power to reverse the decline and build, not only for this generation, but for the generations to come. The walls of faith will be rebuilt so that the Church and nation can be restored and can prosper. There will be opposition; each group will have its Sanballats and Tobiahs who will resent the status quo being upset and will oppose the restoration of the Christian faith. Opposition tests the faith of those being attacked, but when Nehemiah was attacked he stood firm. Those who reject the rebuilding will have no place in the restored Jerusalem, he says. Today those who reject the restoration will themselves miss the opportunity of a lifetime, and they will come to regret it.

What God wants to give us, however, is so much better than what has gone before. To miss the chance to be part of it would be to miss the opportunity of a lifetime. There will be times of waiting, praying and uncertainty, there will be times of testing, there will be times of dynamic action. But led by the Spirit of God, the groups will achieve what the present renewal movements have been unable to do, they will rebuild the walls of faith so that the whole Church and nation will be restored.

In the 1970s Jean Darnell had a picture of this country in darkness. Then lights came on all over the country lighting up the whole scene and spilling over into the rest of Western Europe. This country seems to be part of God's strategy to reach the rest of Western Europe in which Christianity is also in sharp decline. When the Revd John Simons went to the Far East, he kept on coming across Christians who were praying for Britain. When he asked why they were praying for us, they invariably replied, 'Because the Lord has told us to'. His purpose for us is beginning to unfold, but we activist Christians need to be reminded, not once, but over and over again, that it is God's work, not ours, and to be involved we need first and foremost to hear his word to us, and receive from him what he wants us to have and to give to others. Then we will be able to say like the Israelites of Nehemiah's time 'Let us rebuild' and go to it with a will. The ruins of Christianity in Europe lie all around us. The rubble is there for all to see, only by the grace and power of God can the walls of faith be rebuilt, but I believe that now is God's time when he will enable those who are willing to do this work.

So remember, relax and receive first, then you will be able to go out and live the life of faith. You can only give what you have first received from God; the more you receive, the more you will be able to give.

Our own efforts are powerless in the present situation and our own gifts will not really help others. We need to move in God's strength, not our own, and be a channel through which God can give his gifts to others. This is a hard lesson for this self-centred age to learn, but it is the only way in which the walls of faith will really get rebuilt, and with them the Church and nation.

A Prayer for Rebuilding

Heavenly Father, thank you that your love never fails.
We praise you for your loving purposes for our lives,
we ask you for the gift of faith to sustain us,
the gift of the Holy Spirit to lead and empower us.
Help us to receive all that you want to give us,
please help us to give what we have received from you to others,

so that together our faith may be built up, your
will be done,
and Jesus glorified.
Amen.

Study

BIBLE READING: NEHEMIAH 2

QUESTIONS FOR MEDITATION/DISCUSSION

1. What has chapter 2 to tell us about waiting for
   the right moment?
2. What has chapter 2 to tell us about rebuilding
   the walls of faith?
3. How can you and your church be involved in
   rebuilding the walls of faith? (If in a group, make
   a list on a wallchart as a reference.)

PRAYER

After a time of waiting on God in silence, pray about
what he seems to be saying to you about rebuilding
the walls of faith, finishing with the prayer for
rebuilding at the end of chapter 2.

3

Groups to Rebuild

In chapter 3 of the book of Nehemiah we are taken on a tour of the walls of Jerusalem and told who rebuilt each section of them. On a superficial reading of the chapter we might dismiss it as a boring list of names of people we know nothing about, but a closer study tells us some interesting things which are relevant to our situation today.

First of all, many people helped to do the work of rebuilding the wall, the towers and the gates, and because, except for the nobles of Tekoa who get a permanent black mark in the Bible, they all did their bit, the work got done. It was a communal effort, by people outside Jerusalem, as well as those in it. The high priest Eliashib and his fellow priests set the example by rebuilding the sheep gate and the adjacent walls. Later on in the chapter we learn that they also repaired the walls opposite their houses, so they made a significant contribution to the work. The Levites also lent a hand with the rebuilding, as did a group of temple servants. The rest was done by groups of people; sometimes we are only told the leaders' names, but groups such as the goldsmiths and the merchants did their bit, and also residents from the surrounding countryside. Some citizens of

Jerusalem just rebuilt the section opposite their own home. One man was helped by his daughters, another by his sons. The men of Tekoa, as if to make up for their nobles' refusal to take part, repaired two sections of the wall. Between them all the work was accomplished remarkably quickly.

They set to with a will because they knew that their lives literally depended on it. The population of Jerusalem at this time was tiny compared with the task they had to undertake, but with the help of their neighbours and with what must have been a supreme effort they accomplished it.

The task of rebuilding the walls of faith in this country is an immeasurably greater one than the inhabitants of Jerusalem faced in 445 BC. In contrast to the small workforce at Nehemiah's disposal, today there are many groups of people in existence who are capable of doing this work, with God's help. Many years ago now I read a book called *Growth Groups** which gave a clue to how the personal and spiritual development of Christians could be helped to enable them to grow. Rereading it recently confirmed to me that this book showed a practical way forward, through which the walls of faith could be rebuilt, in individuals, in the Church, and in society. If we are to grow in faith, we must live the life of faith, but we need to do so in community, and Howard Clinebell's groups provide a basis for this.

Any biologist or botanist will confirm that a characteristic of all living things is that they grow. The characteristic of Christians who are truly alive is also that they are growing, spiritually and as per-

*Howard Clinebell (Abingdon, 1977).

28

sonalities. One Sunday service a week is not enough to help us to grow, however, and the many tasks and church committees that we can get drafted into are not growth points either. To grow we need to be able to give and receive at deeper levels than are usual in church circles. Most churches are communities of strangers who only communicate at a superficial level. We need a group of people whom we respect and trust, and with whom we can communicate at a level which helps us to change and grow.

So what are growth groups, and how can they help in the task of rebuilding the walls of faith?

First of all they are not necessarily church groups, they can be secular ones – groups of not less than five and not more than eight people, who can meet together around a particular task or theme to help each other. They could be youth groups which help the young people to find their personal identity, preparation for marriage groups, marriage enrichment groups, different age groups, singles' groups, study groups, creativity groups, and so on. The essential ingredient is that people meet to help each other, to free each other to be who they really are. They are not therapy groups: people with big problems need individual ministry to help them on a one-to-one basis. Otherwise there is a danger that they will impede the growth group by hijacking the agenda, and turning the attention of the group onto themselves all the time. *Growth groups are to help well people to function better*. I am referring to spiritual growth groups which can help people to grow in their faith so that they in their turn can help others.

It is necessary for a growth group to meet at least once a week for one and a half to two hours, and in

addition from time to time to spend longer together
– for example, a three to six hour meeting perhaps
starting with a snack meal, or an all-day meeting. A
weekend away will consolidate the work of the
group, but even twenty-four hours away can achieve
a remarkable amount.

A few months ago I was part of a group like this
which came together to talk and pray about the way
forward. We were all in the 'same boat' in that we
all felt called to a ministry that was wider than the
ordinary parish niche, and for which there was no
obvious place in the Church structure. We had found
that our faith was being tested by what we were
going through in our lives, but that as we met and
prayed together the problems were one by one being
sorted out, and our faith built up.

Like many growth groups we started with a
honeymoon period, when we found it refreshing just
to be together. We felt led to commit ourselves to
one another in the Lord for whatever he had for us
to do for him. Then we went through a rather 'flat'
period, when nothing much seemed to be happening
– we seemed rather like a sailing ship becalmed for
lack of wind. But this was a prelude to a sharing
with one another at a deeper level than before, an
ability to share things that are not normally discussed outside the family. This enabled us to help
and liberate each other in the nitty-gritty, the reality
of our daily lives, and meant that we had really
started to do the work of a growth group. Although
we frequently refer to the Bible, we are not a Bible
study group as such. Although we pray each time
we meet, we are not just another prayer group.
Although we have fellowship together, we are not

simply a fellowship group, which could meet on an entirely different level. Not that there is anything wrong with these kinds of groups, they all have a part to play in the church's life, but they are not necessarily growth groups in the sense I am speaking of.

In order to function well as a growth group, it is necessary to have the kind of leadership that facilitates the growth of the group. When the growth of the group is blocked, it is usually because the leadership is too overbearing and dominant, and is stifling the creativity of the group. It is not a vehicle for so-called 'heavy shepherding', i.e. telling people how to live their lives, but helping them to cope with the reality of their lives, and also to respond to the call of God to live and grow in his will. It is God, the Holy Spirit, who should be inspiring the group, guiding them and strengthening them; the leadership should facilitate this process, and progressively the group should take on the leadership tasks.

My own group is being given a vision of running a centre where people can come for ministry and from which we can go out, as individuals and as a ministry team, concerned with renewal, evangelism and the rebuilding of the Church. So we understand the time of testing that we are going through now, as a preparation for that work, not just a way of finding personal self-fulfilment. God's vision is always immensely greater than ours, and if we are obedient to his leading we will find ourselves guided to something greater than ourselves. But, as I said in the previous chapter, we need first to receive from him, as individuals, in the context of a group who are searching with us. Both individually and collectively we need to wait on him, and pursue with him what he wants to do with our lives. As he builds our faith in him, we are enabled to build the faith of others, to give away what God is giving us, in our own prayer life and in the group.

A word of warning though: this help must not turn into tyranny; the group must help each member to find freedom, not to be dominated by the opinions of the group. This needs emotional maturity on the part of all concerned, sensitive leadership, and requires that each person maintain an active relationship with God through their private prayer life. I have found that those who lean too heavily on the ministry of others usually do so because they are not doing the work of prayer in their own lives. Spiritual growth groups work well if those taking part are living a close relationship with God in their own right, can listen as well as speak, give as well as receive. Today many people have very low self-esteem, and find it difficult to resist what is inappropriate from other people. They need building up, but most of all they need to know at a deep level that they are loved as they are by God. A healthy growth group will reinforce that knowledge, and the knowledge that all is well if we are seeking his will. As Jesus says, those who seek will find. So we can be confident that he will reveal to us, if we ask him, what his will is for our lives.

What is needed in terms of leadership and membership, if we wish to set up a spiritual growth group? Howard Clinebell, in his book *Growth Groups*, puts forward the following characteristics necessary for growth group leaders:

(1) they are loving and non-manipulative in relationships;
(2) they are in touch with their own feelings, including any negative ones;
(3) they are open to new ideas and relationships;
(4) they are characterised by sincerity;
(5) their self-esteem is firm;
(6) they can listen to other people.

The members should exhibit the following:

(1) the ability to make good working relationships;
(2) good self-esteem;
(3) a desire to improve relationships;
(4) a wish to grow spiritually;
(5) a wish to use their talents.

It is important that the leader sensitively guides the group through the different levels of sharing, not jumping in straightaway at the deep end, but gradually leading the group to deeper levels of sharing as the level of trust grows, and this becomes appropriate. This can be done by the leader progressively sharing and opening up his or her own life as the group develops. Here is the list of levels of sharing that Howard Clinebell gives, with the reminder that the deeper the sharing goes, the more threatening it becomes.

Least threatening Level 1 – Discussing ideas, information, theories, generalisations.

Level 2 – Sharing personal

experiences from the past.

Level 3 – Sharing current problems and feelings from outside the group.

Level 4 – Encountering the here-and-now relationships and feelings in the group.

Most threatening Level 5 – Sharing very personal problems not ordinarily discussed outside the family.

Howard Clinebell gives a word of warning, 'Anyone who is growing and open poses a threat to those who have made a virtue of their private prisons' (p. 46). If most of the group wants to go deeper but there are individuals for whom this is too threatening, it may be that they would feel more comfortable in a fellowship group that functions only at levels 1, 2 or 3. But the deeper the group feels able to go without overloading the 'feeling circuits', the more help it will be in dealing with the real problems within the group. And those need to be dealt with if we are to grow in faith. God seems to be only interested in us when we are 'real', he is not one to play games with us.

If the group is able to work together harmoniously, and forms a progressive growth group, it will be able to move on to become a ministry team, which is not just facilitating those within the group, but can minister to others in whatever way God leads them.

My own group is called the 'Fivefold Ministry
Fellowship' because we believe that we hold
amongst ourselves the fivefold ministry as in Ephesians 4:11–13:

It was he [Jesus Christ] who gave some to be apostles, some to be prophets, some to be evangelists,
and some to be pastors and teachers, to prepare
God's people for works of service, so that the body
of Christ may be built up until we all reach unity
in the faith and in the knowledge of the Son of
God and become mature, attaining to the whole
measure of the fullness of Christ.

The apostolic gift is necessary in order to build
new community. It is evident from George Carey's
book *Sharing a Vision*,* a collection of the Archbishop's articles and addresses, that he possesses this
gift: he is continually seeking to build community,
both as leader of the Church and also as a national
leader in our wider society. We need modern apostles
like him who can be at the forefront of the rebuilding
of the walls of faith and the rebuilding of society.

If we are to seek God's will we also need those
with a prophetic gift, i.e. those who are able to hear
and communicate what God is saying in our situation today. These are usually the prayer warriors,
who spend time listening to God as well as praying
to him about the situation in which they are set.

In a nation that has fallen away from belief, we
also need evangelists who can get alongside people
and build up their faith in God. Both within the

*Published by Darton, Longman and Todd, 1993.

Church and outside it we need to hear the Good
News and also see it bringing fruit for God's Kingdom. In a missionary situation God is raising up
evangelists among us to undertake this task.

To care for the community we need pastors with
a deeply caring heart for the people, who are not
just interested in filling pews, but who are gifted
with healing and reconciling gifts that will enable
individuals to be liberated into real spiritual freedom
and wholeness. They are shepherds and overseers of
the gathered flock.

In an age of widespread ignorance about the
Christian gospel we also need good teachers to communicate the faith both inside and outside the
Church. Too often we have been satisfied to offer a
watered-down faith, a lowest common denominator
that we hope people can adhere to, instead of building up true faith to a level that can enable God
to work in people's lives. Even Jesus was unable to
work where there was little faith.

The Fivefold Ministry Fellowship believes that
God wants to rebuild his Church based on the fivefold gifts with Jesus Christ as our cornerstone. Our
mission statement is drawn from Isaiah 61:1–4:

The Spirit of the Sovereign Lord is on me,
because the Lord has anointed me
to preach good news to the poor.
He has sent me to bind up the broken-hearted,
to proclaim freedom for the captives
and release from darkness for the prisoners,
to proclaim the year of the Lord's favour
and the day of vengeance of our God,
to comfort all who mourn,

and provide for those who grieve in Zion –
to bestow on them a crown of beauty instead of
    ashes,
the oil of gladness instead of mourning,
and a garment of praise instead of a spirit of
    despair.
They will be called oaks of righteousness,
a planting of the Lord for the display of his
    splendour.
They will rebuild the ancient ruins
and restore the places long devastated;
they will renew the ruined cities
that have been devastated for generations.

This is Jesus' mission (Luke 4:16–21), but it is also ours, in that we, anointed by God's Holy Spirit, feel called to minister to the poor and hurting, and to a deliverance ministry for those who are captive, so that they, restored by the Lord, will go out and join in the task of rebuilding the walls of faith, rebuilding the Church and also our society.

We need many groups like this all over the country, each dedicated to rebuilding the part of the wall they are called by God to do.

It is noticeable that in Nehemiah 3 the Israelites start by building the gates, then they build the walls. It is as important that people find their way into the Kingdom society where God's will is done, as it is to keep the enemy out. We need ways to come in and go out, as well as walls of protection. As each group seeks God's will, it will be led to that portion of rebuilding that he is calling them to. It will be a communal effort, and not only the life of the individuals and groups taking part but also the life of the Church and nation depend on it. God is already calling groups into being to be employed on this task. We need everyone who is called to say, like the people of Jerusalem, 'Let us rebuild'.

'But aren't we rebuilding already?' some will ask. 'The job of the Church is to build the walls of faith, and we are doing this surely?' In answer to that I would say that most of the effort we put into our faith at present is required to keep up the status quo. But the status quo is not outward-looking enough, and the current rate of growth is too small to make any impact on the present situation. The efforts of people in renewal are often marginalised and concerned with building a Church community that can be inward-looking. All too frequently they fail to help to rebuild the walls of faith in our wider society. This country has never been one hundred per cent Christian, but a really active and committed ten per cent of the population who have been liberated by the Spirit of God and are growing would change society – these Christians would truly be salt, light and leaven in the wider society as they are called to be. What I am speaking of is a movement of God's Spirit that will alter the status quo, and set us on the path of recovering our faith, so that the Church and nation will be rebuilt. This is a huge task, but not too great for the Lord, who will, I believe, work through small groups of people to accomplish his aim.

As in chapter 3 of Nehemiah, we will, I believe, have the help of people from other nations who will aid us in the task. We have been used in this country to sending our missionaries abroad. Already this trend is being reversed, and we have begun to receive missionaries from lands overseas where faith is flourishing, to come and help in the restoration here. It is God's sovereign work from start to finish, but he works through people, and together the work can be done, together with each other, and together with the Spirit of God.

Holy Spirit, we ask you to inspire and guide us,
rebuild our faith in the Father and the Son,
so that together we may build the walls of faith,
to restore our Church and nation.
We ask this in Jesus' name
and for his honour and glory.
Amen.

Study

BIBLE READING: NEHEMIAH 3

QUESTIONS FOR MEDITATION/DISCUSSION

1. What does Nehemiah 3 have to tell us about working together in community?
2. How can we help each other to grow in faith?
3. How can we work together to rebuild the walls of faith?

PRAYER

After a time of waiting on God in silence, pray for each other and for the church and community to which you belong. Finish with the prayer at the end of this chapter.

4

Dealing with Opposition

In chapters 4 and 6 of the book of Nehemiah we have an account of opposition to the rebuilding of the wall of Jerusalem. In chapter 4 Sanballat and Tobiah, whom we met for the first time in chapter 2, are furious to find the rebuilding going ahead, and pour scorn on the whole enterprise. Tobiah says sarcastically that even a fox climbing up on the wall would break it down. Nehemiah prays that God will fight them on his behalf and carries on with the rebuilding, and the people work 'with all their heart'. When the wall reaches half its planned height, Sanballat and Tobiah are incensed, and plot together with the Arabs, the Ammonites and the men of Ashdod to come and fight to stop it being completed. The people of Judah speak against it. Nehemiah arms half the men so that they can guard the other half while they are working. The builders carry swords and other weapons too. Nehemiah encourages his people, and they carry on building the wall.

In chapter 6, Sanballat and Tobiah try to trick Nehemiah into coming out of Jerusalem to meet them. When this fails, they send an unsealed letter accusing him of rebellion and plotting to become king, all of which Nehemiah refutes strongly. Then

Shemaiah, who is in the pay of Sanballat and Tobiah, tries to trick Nehemiah into taking refuge in the temple. Nehemiah, as a layman, is not allowed into the temple, and would have been infringing the Law of God if he had sought to enter it, so he refuses. In spite of the attempts of the enemy the wall is rebuilt in record time, fifty-two days. Nevertheless opposition still continues, and Tobiah keeps sending letters to try to intimidate Nehemiah.

Whenever there is an advance for the Kingdom of God, there will be opposition.

I have found that it is at the times in my life when spiritual progress is being made, for example at my conversion and at times of spiritual renewal and revival, that opposition has been at its most intense. There will be no rebuilding of the walls of faith without opposition; we must expect it to come – everything from ridicule to outright attack. Jesus said that we are blessed when we receive insults and rejection for his sake: more than that he says, 'Woe to you when all men speak well of you' (Luke 6:26). Like Nehemiah, when opposition comes, we need to have prayer warriors fighting the spiritual battle if progress is to continue. We need the full armour of God if we are to engage in this spiritual fight. Because the battle is not just with individuals or groups, but against the forces of evil which are trying to frustrate the advance of the Kingdom of God. St Paul says,

... Be strong in the Lord and in his mighty power. Put on the full armour of God so that you can take your stand against the devil's schemes. For our struggle is not against flesh and blood, but against the rulers, against the authorities, against the powers of this dark world and against the spiritual forces of evil in the heavenly realms. Therefore put on the full armour of God, so that when the day of evil comes, you may be able to stand your ground, and after you have done everything, to stand. (Ephesians 6:10–13)

Nehemiah stands his ground, and is not deflected from his purpose, but he takes precautions, and he is worldly wise when his enemies try to trick him. No naïvety then, and no accommodation with the enemy, but a strong, firm leadership carries the work forward to completion.

This is easier said than done for clergy nowadays. The Church today is divided about so many issues that it is difficult for clergy to move their people forward while keeping them together. This is particularly true when it comes to renewing the church. Alongside renewalists who want change and want to move forward, there are traditionalists who often do not want any change whatsoever, and it is difficult, to say the least, to please both groups.

It has been estimated that seventy per cent of ordinands have had a charismatic experience, but they find it difficult to share their experience with their parishes.

An example of how clergy have to battle against opposition was given to me by Prebendary John Simons, Rector of Holy Trinity, Nailsea, and chairman of Bath and Wells Diocesan Renewal Group. John comes from the evangelical wing of the Anglican Church, but is not partisan about narrow issues of churchmanship. Nothing in his life has transcended the original experience of being born again, despite the fact that his conversion brought opposition from within his family, and was also questioned by two professional people whose opinion mattered to John. Providentially he was given a book by Martin Lloyd-Jones entitled *Conversion, Spiritual and Psychological* which answered the questions his medical friends had raised, and reassured him. But John's father was so alienated by his conversion that he refused to come to his wedding. Happily their relationship was restored and strengthened at a later date.

While John was at theological college, his wife Jenny was working up in the City, and needed to catch an early train, so she used to go and have her quiet time in one of the City churches. While she was there one day she had a quite wonderful experience of God's presence, and found herself speaking in tongues. This experience was at first rejected by her husband, who from his 'lofty pinnacle as a theological student' took the stance that this was very dangerous, and poured a big douche of cold water on it. She stood firm, however, but had to bide her time until John was able to follow where she had led. Like many people, John did not find it easy to come into charismatic gifts because he was very suspicious about self-deception. At St Andrew's, Chorleywood, however, where he was assigned as a student, Edgar Trout led him into a charismatic experience of speaking in tongues, which finally convinced him.

When as a result he and Jenny became involved in renewal circles, he became aware that in the Evangelical church from which he emanated this was not regarded as 'sound'.

There was an unspoken sense that they had gone off the rails. He managed to live with this, but there was a sadness not to be in tune with people who had meant a good deal to Jenny and to him. Since then these issues have been largely worked through, and some Conservative Evangelicals have come to accept charismatic experience. There has been a change in climate, but these divisions were particularly difficult in the sixties.

Leaving theological college, John had to cope with the issue of being open to parishes about his charismatic stance. His first vicar, although not hostile, was cautious because of a bad experience of renewal he had had previously. So as curate John had to lie low and not give expression to his full spirituality. Again, he felt sad that he could not share this. In all he had to keep his charismatic experience on a back burner through theological college, through curacy, and through the first two years of being a vicar – in all, seven or eight years. Many ordinands are in a similar position.

John's first church as an incumbent was at St Luke's, Cranham, in Essex. There had been problems before they went there, which meant that the congregation had dwindled to about twenty-five to thirty people. The positive side of this was that they could start from scratch. He was put under a lot of pressure by the bishop to adopt a more middle-of-the-road churchmanship, but he stood firm. To begin with there was a need to get to know people. It was a case of watering what was already there, and praying for increase. The increase mainly came through con-

version growth. Many people became Christians.
Because they were new Christians, they were very
teachable and open to the Holy Spirit, keen to share
their faith, and generous in giving. The charismatic
dimension came in naturally as the church grew,
numerically and spiritually. The congregation
increased to around 200–250 people. To be in such a
young growing church was a delight and a privilege.

When they came to Nailsea, however, John and
Jenny found that bringing the church there to
renewal was without doubt to prove the most painful
experience they had ever had. There were a number
of Christians who wanted to forge ahead with the
Lord, and there was a sense of expectancy that a new
vicar would mark a new chapter in the life of the
church. There was also a strong contingent of more
traditional Christians. So within the church there
were strong elements both for change and against
change. When it became apparent that John and
Jenny felt some changes were necessary, battle lines
were drawn, with John and Jenny in the middle, and
this was a very painful place to be.

John felt that the church had to diversify if it was
to meet the needs of those who wanted to move
forward, and also bring God's love to people who
were outside the church. Many were interested in
becoming Christians, but would not join the church
if it were in too much of a traditional strait-jacket.
From the outset, it was always his conviction that if
the parish was to diversify, they should not concentrate just on mainly informal services, but should
retain the traditional ones also. He is puzzled by
churches who say that they cannot change. He
believes that a church can have a spectrum of

services, and meet the preferences and aspirations of different groups of people on any one Sunday. Polarisation is not the only option.

However, although John believes in that philosophy of change which takes diversity into account, implementing it was quite another matter. Once the honeymoon period was over, he found that there were some Christians whose loyalty was to the traditional spirituality in which they had been nurtured, and which they did not want to see disturbed, while there were others who wanted to move on, and looked to him to be an agent of that change. Setting a pace that was fair to both camps in the diversification was difficult. Some people were lost at both ends of the spectrum.

John did not feel that he should launch in with both barrels firing, but should try to introduce change gently and reassure those who wanted change that things were moving, and those who wanted things to stay as they were, that they were cared for and that there would still be a pattern of worship on Sundays that gave them what they were looking for. In fact he did not succeed in satisfying either side, with the result that those who did not want change pulled out and went to a local church that could meet their preferences. Those who wanted the church to move on into renewal became impatient with the pace he had felt it right to set, pulled out and went to renewed churches elsewhere, or the House Churches. That was a very painful time, when John experienced both the brickbats and the bouquets that go with being a vicar.

Previously John had encountered clergy who felt that they had come into the ministry with a real vision and call from God. Then something seems to have happened and they had gone 'off the boil'. He had never quite understood before why that had happened. When he experienced the mounting of all the pressures at Nailsea, he began to understand, and saw that here were clergy who were seeking to be obedient to a vision that God had given them, had tried to implement it, and then 'sparks flew'. Things became so painful for both him and Jenny, that in the end, having given it their best shot, they either had to shoulder all the pain, or compromise and settle for what they had got. He now understood better what had happened to his fellow clergy, because he had been there too. He and Jenny only survived by the skin of their teeth through the care of a few families who really understood what they were attempting and took the trouble to come round and say, 'John, we know what you are going through, we are with you, don't give up!' That was just enough to see them through. He would not be disparaging of anybody who found trying to introduce change so painful that it became unbearable.

When he had taken the baton over from his hard-working predecessor John had felt that it was necessary to draw people together into a family. So he went in for some bridge-building innovations such as introducing coffee at the back of the church, and home groups as ways to help people to get to know each other more closely. Later, after initial difficulties which were solved by appointing a lay-pastor to look after the home group leaders, the number of people meeting regularly in home groups grew to be about two hundred. Faith-sharing teams from other churches came in and explained what was happening with them. He got to a stage where he felt that the seeds of renewal were present, but not yet the fruits of it.

One day he was out visiting, and someone said to him, 'Please don't take offence, but when I was praying for you the other day I felt the Lord say to me that John is being handicapped by fear of men.' John was surprised, yet quickly felt that such a cap fitted. He was quite bothered by what people in the parish thought of the innovative things that were in his heart to do and by what the ecclesiastical hierarchy thought about it. He felt the Lord challenging him about this fear of other people's opinions of him.

Soon after he went to a John Wimber conference at Brighton, and prayed to the Lord about this matter while he was there. At a particular point in the conference he responded to an invitation to clergy to go forward to rededicate their ministry, so he sought to say to the Lord, 'From now on, if you are my helper, I will try not to be getting in your way through fearing what other people think of me, rather than what you think of me.' In response to his prayer he had an extraordinarily powerful experience of being refilled with the Holy Spirit. He came back from that to a parish weekend, and shared with the church what had happened to him.

What happened as a result was out of all proportion to what he could have expected. Many in the congregation were filled with the Spirit, as was a visiting evangelism team, and the whole church moved ahead as a result. It really was a pivotal point which moved the church more fully into renewal.

When renewal came, they wondered how to express it in worship. It was a time when many

people were leaving the Church of England and joining the House Churches. A national leader visited
Nailsea and challenged John and a curate colleague
as to whether they should really be in the Church
of England. They both answered 'yes'. The visiting
speaker had real reservations about the compromises
being made in the Church of England, and the time
that renewal took. John and his colleague both said,
'Well, if we have got it wrong we shall both have to
say sorry to God, but we feel called to be in the
Church of England.' Although dramatic things do
not happen every day, they could look around the
church on a Sunday and see this family that used
not to come to church and now are born again, that
family that are now committed and really serving
God. The pace may be slow, but the fruits of the
Spirit are evident. Those within the congregation
who were impatient with the Anglican setting challenged the status quo. The staff and the PCC came
to the conclusion after some heart-searching that
they were an Anglican church, they were committed
to being an Anglican church, and with the freedom
they had 'within the framework' they were not
ashamed of being Anglican, because that is what
God had called them to be. This brought rejection
from those who tended more towards the House
Church style of worship and they lost some people
who were not happy with this stand.

John describes the dynamics of trying to navigate
a course through so many rocks and rapids as
'interesting' – it was a case of standing one's ground
and realising from time to time that people are not
going to like it.

What enabled him to stand his ground, as well as

the support he received from some of the congregation, was the vision that God had put into his heart, which like Nehemiah he had kept to himself for some time. '... I had not told anyone what my God had put in my heart to do for Jerusalem' (2:12). This has always been an important Scripture for John.

John believes that God can put something into a person's heart, and the recipient knows without a shadow of doubt that God has put it there. Over the years John has had convictions about the daily use of Scripture, and the daily work of prayer as the key to our relationship with God. Although he feels that he puts on 'L' plates every day when he prays, and every New Year when he recommits himself to the Lord, the conviction has never left him that God has put some things into his heart that he needs to fulfil. He has stood up and been counted on the things that he feels are from God. For example, he was convinced that God wanted him to go and see George Carey, when he was Bishop of Bath and Wells, to ask him about starting a Diocesan Renewal Group. He received warm encouragement from the then future Archbishop, but has attracted flak from some other quarters. However, he has not been deflected from his commitment because of his compact with the Lord. John feels it is important to hear from people. He listens hard to what people say. Leadership cannot afford to be isolated or dictatorial: a test of one's conviction makes it stronger and at other times there is something to learn or modify.

'In the counsel of many, right things are established' (Proverbs 15:22). This truth has helped him to be more broad shouldered about the criticisms and disapprovals that there have been. It remains important to him to have the approval of those whom he can respect and hopefully to win their support, but in the final analysis, he knows he needs to stand by his convictions.

He sees the regular central prayer meetings of the church as most important. Prayer is vital in the spiritual battle. We are given authority in Jesus' name to render the powers of darkness useless. The Greek word *katargeo* describes this perfectly. It means to reduce to ineffectiveness. It is like drawing the pin from a hand grenade, so that it becomes ineffective. This is also what the powers of darkness are trying to do to the Church, (and also what the Church is called to do to Satan: 'Bind the strong man', so that the captives can be released, see Matthew 12:29). So the battle is on to raise dissension, to get us to be disobedient, to waylay us with man-made agendas rather than addressing the issues to which the Spirit is directing – any way whatever in which we can be rendered ineffective. In this battle the use of Scripture and intercessory prayer is vital.

Though much of what goes wrong is due to human sinfulness or failure, the devil constantly tries to exacerbate those things. The battle lines are drawn in these matters. Clear thinking and spiritual discernment are needed to distinguish the right way forward when there are problems. It may be that wise counsel is required, or maybe a person needs inner healing, or there may be demonic influence. It is essential to have the right remedy – it is useless to give wise counsel if deliverance ministry is needed; on the other hand there is no point in fighting demons if wise counsel or inner healing is required.

There is a theatre of warfare and these three lines of explanation must not be blurred. To be aware of the battle is only the beginning. If any one of these three spiritual 'remedies' is lacking, it can result in people being reduced to ineffectiveness.

If the Greek word *katargeo* sums up what the spiritual battle is all about, the Greek word *hupomoneo* sums up the Christian position. It means to 'abide underneath'. It is true that we dwell in the heavenly places with Christ, but we cannot deny that we also dwell under spiritual attack and suffering. We hold both conditions. Like the disciples we can be up on the mountain of Transfiguration at one moment, but also down in the valleys with the demonic child at the next. There is a need for patience and long-suffering in the valleys. We need stickability.

It has been a long haul, but John has seen many of the things that God put on his heart, right at the beginning of his ministry, bear fruit. His desire to share renewal has resulted in a measure of continuing renewal in his parish, and the setting up and operating of the Diocesan Renewal Group in Bath and Wells. His concern for World Mission and his belief that short-term mission visits are effective have led to him becoming chairman of SOMA (UK) (Sharing of Ministries Abroad). His conviction that prayer is vital and that the spiritual temperature of the nation can be changed by intercessory prayer, has led to the setting up of Cross-winds (see chapter 1). The cost has been that of having to deal with a degree of opposition, right from the beginning of his days as a Christian, which has intensified as each initiative began to take off. His experience is a vivid illustration of the kinds of pressure we can expect if we are to build the walls of faith. The divisions that John found when he came to Nailsea are in existence right across the Church, and are to be found in most parishes. We need patience and stickability, long-suffering and deep conviction if the task of rebuilding the walls of faith is to be accomplished, but like Nehemiah, we shall find that it can be done if we are not deterred from the task and if, like the people of Jerusalem, we 'work with all our heart'.

If you visit Holy Trinity, Nailsea today, you will find a thriving church with 500 adults, 300 children and young people, six full-time and two part-time staff, an eldership team and a recently planted church in a housing estate. You might not guess that so much pain lies behind what appears to be on the surface a straightforward success story.

John, however, while grateful for what God has built, sees the church as 'Work-In-Progress' and not remotely any kind of finished product. He recognises both the unsolved flaws and problems, and the many opportunities that beckon ahead. His hope is that the best is yet to come.

Holy Trinity, Nailsea has the vital ingredients that are needed for the renewing of a church: a leadership with a strong vision of what God wants to do with that church, and the willingness to stick with the vision through all the difficulties that the church has encountered. The cost is high, but the reward is great. There is only one joy that is greater than seeing someone being born again in Christ, and that is the joy of seeing an entire community being born again, being renewed by the Holy Spirit, and receiving new life. May it be so in our Church and nation.

Collect for the Fourth Sunday after Epiphany

Almighty God,
in Christ you make all things new.
Transform the poverty of our nature
by the riches of your grace,
and in the renewal of our lives
make known your heavenly glory;
through Jesus Christ our Lord.

Amen.*

Study

BIBLE READING: NEHEMIAH 4 AND 6

QUESTIONS FOR MEDITATION/DISCUSSION

1. What does Nehemiah have to show us about leading a project in spite of opposition?
2. What does John Simons' account have to tell us about the renewal of the Church?
3. How can a church move forward when there are conflicting opinions in the membership?

PRAYER

Pray for the rebuilding of the walls of faith, ending with the Collect at the end of the chapter.

*Taken from *The Alternative Service Book 1980*.

54

5

Social Responsibility

During the rebuilding of the walls of Jerusalem, Nehemiah faces an economic crisis which brings the work to a halt. There is a famine and the Jews suffering under it begin to cry out against their fellow Jews. They complain that they have had to borrow money to get grain and also to pay the king's taxes. Because they have been unable to pay back the money, the lenders have sold them and their sons and daughters into slavery. This was against the Law of Moses: the Jews were not allowed to enslave their fellow countrymen and women. Nehemiah is very angry to hear what is going on, and calls a public meeting. He accuses the nobles and officials of selling their brothers into slavery, and they have no answer to this complaint. He tells them to give back immediately the fields, vineyards, olive groves and houses that they have possessed, and also to reimburse the interest that they have been charging. They agree, and take an oath to do what they have promised.

Nehemiah points out that he did not take advantage of his position as governor to make money or to 'lord it over the people'. Instead he concentrated on building the wall, and employed his own men on the project. Also he fed the people from his own resources instead of taking food from them or acquiring land. There is no false modesty here, Nehemiah has set an example to his people, and this is probably the reason why they obey him without demur.

The commentary in the NIV Study Bible points out that the economic crisis was probably caused by the exaction of taxes by the Persians, as well as by the famine.

The acquisition of land by the Persians, taking it out of food production, also fuelled inflation which reached fifty per cent. The combination of these economic pressures was pushing some of the Jews back into the slavery from which they had only just been redeemed! Nehemiah's example shows that there was an alternative to oppressing the people in this way, since they could be fed from the resources that were available. The building of the walls took second place while this crisis was sorted out; there could be no renewed society based on injustice. The protection of the city by new walls would be of little avail if God's Law was not being obeyed within them.

Rereading this chapter immediately brought to mind the position that we are in now in respect to Third World debt. The developed world has been lending sums of money to the Third World at a rate which they are unable to repay. Just paying the interest is driving these nations into even deeper poverty and debt. If they mortgage all their crops they still cannot manage to repay the debts, and the interest goes on rising. Even when we give help to the Third World there are strings attached which cause difficulty. A prize example is that of a dam which has never worked. All the planning work carried out in the donor country was calculated on the basis of the evaporation rate in a northern climate, so the water level has never reached the pumps. Very often free gifts are tied to conditions, such as that the maintenance work must be carried out by the donor country. The recipients cannot afford this and so they are forced to go even deeper into debt to service the free gift.

I was much relieved when John Major started talking about forgiving some of these Third World debts, but he does not seem to have got very far because the developed countries have not really taken on board one of the principles of the Brandt Commission in the 1970s. The Commission pointed out that the future of the developing countries will in the long term affect the developed countries. We are a small world, and all the countries are interlinked, even the poorest nations. One of the poorest is Nicaragua. The only way in which their debts to the World Bank can be serviced is by taking out further loans, and these new loans have higher penalties.

Nearer home there is an underclass emerging in this country. In an attempt to tighten up who can receive Social Security benefits, we have reached a situation where the State is returning people who have endeavoured to stand on their own feet, back into the poverty trap and homelessness – in short to the underclass.

Graham Earney, previously the Social Responsibility Officer for the Bath and Wells Diocese, gave me an example of how this can happen. He was involved in a project for housing homeless young people. The project takes people whether they are on Income Support or earning, but encourages them to get jobs. The position of one resident came to the committee responsible for the project because she owed some back rent. She was employed and not eligible for housing benefit. She had been sick, but because she worked part-time she was not eligible either for sickness benefit or for income from her employer. She had been tested for eligibility for housing benefit in a period of five weeks which included Christmas, during which she had worked overtime so that other people could have a holiday. As a result her housing benefit had been withdrawn, without any consideration being given to the fact that she had had no income through sickness. If she had been completely dependent on benefits, she could have survived. However, because she was trying to pay her way with a part-time job, which was all she could get, she was not able to manage. The gains of working had been so marginal that the merest hiccup, like two or three weeks' sickness, had thrown the whole thing out.

The management committee of the housing project made the decision not to repossess this young woman's room because of bad debt, which they could have done legally; they were willing to forgive the debt, because otherwise she would have been forced to return to homelessness. They were able to be flexible; why can't the State be flexible, too? As a matter of justice, the State should stand where the Housing Association which ran this project has. We need to be more merciful, and also more flexible. The Church, too, is used to living with ambiguity about pastoral matters. Where people are concerned, it will never be all straight lines able to be governed by rigid rules. We must be able to adapt to particular circumstances.

In the past decade we have witnessed a total change in the way people are employed. The Industrial Missioners I worked with in the early eighties saw the situation coming in which there would be little or no work for the vast numbers of people who were traditionally employed in unskilled jobs. We have seen the end of the Industrial Revolution, and have moved towards highly technical, skilled jobs which have come with the computer revolution. This has caused a 'shake-out' for millions of people who have lost their jobs through no fault of their own. They were told by Norman Tebbit to get 'on yer bike!' They went but were overwhelmed by the difficulties of life in the big cities. Many came to London, but found themselves homeless on the streets, and unable to get a job because they were homeless.

This trend has contributed to the growth of the traveller movement. Part of the reason for this has been that people caught in the poverty trap have been trying to find a better life. Taking to the streets in the countryside seems a better option than taking to the streets in the concrete jungle.

Some people get to the point where they feel that they are not going to make it in the mainstream, so they opt out of the system and try to find a better quality of life in the countryside.

What has also happened is that market forces have been allowed to dominate, while at the same time a sense of community has been lost. As a result people are less willing to allow their resources to be used for others. We now have no consensus view about how to give to others. This is a collective responsibility for the whole of society and not all down to the government. We get the government we deserve. The Church needs to emphasise the reclaiming of a sense of community. What we need is partnership in the community. Care packages need to be delivered where people can feel at ease and make the best of them, which is at home. However, 'Care in the Community' as a concept has failed because there is a need for cultural change as well as change in government systems.

'Care in the Community' was based on a false set of assumptions about society. The speed with which the large mental institutions were run down has been catastrophic and has caused many casualties. The desire to have people supported in their homes is fine as long as there is the infrastructure to do it. However, people get very worried about individuals with broken minds being brought close to their homes. The potential host community fears those with mental illness and reacts with N.I.M.B.Y. (Not In My Back Yard). The Church needs to be at the forefront of challenging that fear, and preparing people to be reconciled with those who are different. That is the cultural change that is needed if this system is to work. In addition there must be the political and corporate social will to pay for the cost of this to be done. It was hoped that 'Care in the Community' would be a cheap solution, whereas in order for it to work properly we must all be prepared to give.

When I was being trained for management I was told, 'Never let yourself be run by accountants'. But as a nation we seem to be being run by the Treasury, and all decisions seem to be cash-driven. In my own Diocese of Bath and Wells we are fortunate in having a Board of Finance made up of individuals who understand their role as advising on how we can resource decisions which have been made initially on theological grounds. We decide to do a piece of work for God's Kingdom first, and then look at how to resource it. Too often in Church and State, however, the cart is put before the horse.

An example of what happens if your decisions are cash-driven was given to me by Graham Earney. Last year Somerset Probation Service lost five per cent of its budget, which means it will have to make six people redundant, but the remaining staff are still expected to reach the same quality of service. Ironically this is because the Service has reached its target in previous years, and as a result money has gone to authorities that have not met their targets. The Treasury is thus penalising success. Somerset is leading the field – it has the highest rates of non-custodial roles, *and* the highest rates of non re-offending. Because it is leading the field it is being penalised. Its success is being jeopardised because the Treasury has decided to impose cash limits. This is a cash-driven decision, and a nonsense.

Neither of the leading political parties seems to have the answer to this problem. In the past when it was in power the Labour Party spent money that it did not have. The government was thought to have a bottomless pit of money at its disposal, but this turned out not to be the case: they had to go begging to the I.M.F. and the World Bank, and the country had to be bailed out. Maybe the next Labour Party will be different. The Conservatives on the other hand have pursued a cash-driven policy which has accelerated the appearance of the underclass. Neither party seems to have the answer. Nehemiah on the other hand, did not put a burden on the people, he fed them himself.

He showed an example of giving by his leadership, the complete opposite of the directors of privatised companies recently who have been busy feathering their own nests while making some of their workers redundant and holding down the pay of others. Nehemiah says, 'Give back to them [the people] immediately their fields, vineyards, olive groves and houses, and also the usury you are charging them . . .'(5:11). He is returning to the people those things over which they should rightly have control. Both Labour and Tory philosophies are flawed in this respect. Under Labour the State decides and a heavy bureaucracy dominates the people, though new Labour have tried to address this. Under the Tories the market is the arbiter, but the market is never free; it is led by the ethics of those who take part in it, and today's ethics are sharpness and greed. The Scriptures would not support either policy. The people who are sharp and greedy are told not to be, and a balance is kept between individual and collective responsibility.

Nehemiah gives back to the people their realm of choice, and their freedom under the law. This is not just about money and possessions, but about dignity and the right to have a proper part in the decision-making processes. Today we need to give back responsibility from non-attributable quangos to bodies that have accountability. This applies to such things as NHS Trusts, the privatisation of the justice system, and education. Power has been slipping from the democratically elected bodies to these independent bodies, and there are now whole areas of people's lives where their choice is limited.

All these social factors at work in our society have hidden costs – the most prevalent being that the 'feel good' factor has gone. People have become worryingly sceptical about solutions, particularly political solutions. They have stopped feeling that they can believe anybody. Whole areas of our society are in depression, and their world-view has become soured by the doom and gloom news on their television screens that they see every day. In this country the recession of the early nineties reached areas which had previously remained untouched. This has left an uncertainty about the future. We see emerging what in biblical terms one can only call a hunger after righteousness. People seem to be saying, 'We know there is something needed, but we don't know what it is.' Has the redemptive God anything to say to us about this? What is a realistic hope in the present situation? How can the Kingdom of God come in our society?

The task of rebuilding the walls of faith is not so that the Church will prosper once again but in order to help our whole society. People in Jerusalem worked for the benefit of the whole community not just for their own little houses. Those who have confidence in the living God need to share their Christian hope with those who have no faith. Building the walls of faith means supporting those who have to make ethical decisions about the world of work, and the wider community to which we belong. Nehemiah gave his people the ethical and spiritual leadership they needed. We need to pray for our leaders, and also to pray that God will raise up new leaders who under God can rise to the challenge of life today. Nehemiah shows us what is necessary in order to achieve this. The walls of faith need to be rebuilt so that God's will can be done. Within them God's righteousness must be followed. Rebuilding the walls has a vicarious nature. So much of what we do as a Church is self-centred – for example, we build a youth centre in the hope that it will simply draw the young people into church. Instead we need to create a space in which they can find God, themselves and each other.

The people who came to Graham Earney's parish came because they found real answers to their needs; they stayed in thankfulness, and then went out in joy. They knew that something was missing in their lives, and they found in the parish a community of people who helped them to discover what that was. They joined the community of faith, but went out able to change their lives and the lives of others.

In Jerusalem the high priest rebuilt the main gate which made it possible for people to go in and out. The gates seem to have been built first and then the walls between them. They were creating a place with ways in and ways out, not just a ghetto. There is a need today to go out from within the walls of faith and a need to bring people in.

There is no point building the walls of faith unless there is righteous behaviour within them. Nehemiah asks the leaders to behave righteously according to the Law of God, and he himself gives an example of righteous behaviour. People today are revolted by examples of self-seeking, such as the behaviour of the directors of privatised companies. Is this the beginning of a turning back to God's way of doing things? It certainly creates a climate in which people are rejecting sharpness and greed. People are saying, 'This is not right, this is not the way to conduct business, this is not the right way to run a society.' There is hopefully the beginning of a reclaiming of a society run by moral principles rather than cash.

There has been a growth of individualism in our society, a taking of responsibility for our own actions, but we need a public morality, a common rule of ethics. The Church has always seen faith as a matter of living in community under God, not just a matter of individually held opinions. In the book of Nehemiah the sense of the individual and the community are seen as not being mutually exclusive.

We are all unique individuals, but we have to live in the context of society. I cannot with impunity build up myself while causing pain or problems to others. We need each other – we need to listen to those who are suffering as the underclass as they tell us what it means to be human in the 1990s.

Nehemiah undertook the practical task of rebuilding the walls of faith with an undergirding theology and spirituality. He was actually rebuilding society in that place with fundamental religious values. We need to do the same. Rebuilding the walls will be of little worth unless God's will is being done within them, and God requires of us that we treat all our society with justice and equity.

The 'Noon' Prayer

Lord, give us a vision for our country.
May it be a land of justice and peace,
where people do not take unfair advantage of
    each other,
where all have sufficient
and poverty and vice will have no place to fester,
where seeking to serve others
means more than honour and success,
where order does not rest on force,
where faith, hope and love flourish
and all work for the will of God.
In the name of Jesus Christ,
    Amen.

Study

BIBLE READING: NEHEMIAH 5

QUESTIONS FOR MEDITATION/DISCUSSION

1. What does Nehemiah 5 tell us about the principles on which society should be run?
2. Judging by these principles, what is wrong with our own society? (In a group use a wallchart for reference.)
3. What can we as a church do about it?

PRAYER

Pray for our society ending with the Noon Prayer.

For more information about Noon, please write to:
    Noon Ministries
    42 Friar Gate
    Derby DE1 1DA
    Tel: 01332 349409
    Fax: 01332 200185

6

The Faithful Remnant

In chapter 7 we are introduced to the first of two censuses that appear in the book of Nehemiah. The walls have been rebuilt, and the gates replaced. The city is large and spacious, but there are few people living in it. So Nehemiah tells us that God put it into his heart to register the people by families. The whole company numbered 42,360, not including their servants and singers. Chapter 11 is made up of a list of those who were living in Jerusalem. We are told that one out of ten was chosen by lot to come and live in the city. In chapter 12 we are given a list of the names of the priests and Levites who returned from Babylon with Zerubbabel. Nehemiah clearly found it very important to tell us who returned from Babylon, and who among them actually went to live in Jerusalem. They are the faithful remnant of God's people. In times of religious decline, there was always a faithful remnant in Israel who carried on their faith, and this particular group had chosen to return to their home country and be part of the struggle to re-establish the nation after it had been destroyed by the Babylonians. Their names have been recorded for posterity by Nehemiah in tribute to what they had done.

More than twenty years ago now a friend said to me, 'The Church will continue to decline until only a faithful remnant is left.' This has indeed happened – the number of churchgoers has steadily declined ever since the First World War, and recent statistics show that the Church of England now has only just over a million members in all, and is still in decline. That is the same number as belong to the Evangelical Alliance.

The Roman Catholic Church claims to have three million members, but that includes everyone alive who has been baptised into the Roman Catholic Church in this country, whether they are practising Christians or not, whereas the Church of England and the Evangelical Alliance only count the active membership who are actually in church on Sundays, so the figures are not comparable.

Looking at the Church of England, only 2.3 per cent of the population are actually in church on a Sunday, despite the fact that it claims to be the national State Church of this country. But to presume from this statistic that the Church of England is dead or dying would be a mistake. There are areas that are dying, and areas that are humming with life. Generally speaking it is the traditional middle-of-the-road churches that are in decline, and the Evangelical and particularly the Evangelical Charismatic churches that are humming with life. The traditionalist churches tend to be in great difficulty, whereas the spiritually renewed churches are often growing and planting new churches. What does this mean for the Churches in this country, all of which are experiencing the renewalist/traditionalist split, but particularly for the Church of England? On one hand, there is sharp decline with churches dying, while on the other hand there are overflowing churches which are planting on average one new church every fortnight, though the increase in membership of the renewed churches is still not significant enough to redress the general decline.

I talked to the Revd Patrick Revell, who is Rural Dean of two very traditional deaneries in a mainly rural population. The rural churches tend to be the most conservative, and it is much more difficult to renew them than churches in the urban setting. There had been a census recently (1955) of church attendance on three Sundays, and Patrick Revell had the figures. These figures had shocked the clergy chapter when he had first shared them with them. Here is a sample of the kinds of congregation these country churches were getting: 10, 8, 11, 9, 18, 17, 10, 14, 14, 30, 30, 10, 15, 31, 11, 20, 12. The church attendance has dropped, but the decline was less marked in the smaller parishes than in the larger ones. In all there were forty churches for six hundred people, which gives an average of about fifteen people per church. Patrick Revell felt that this was a nonsense and could not continue. The problem is that the churches are drawing on an ageing population with no replacements coming in. People are not seeing worship as relevant to their lives. For a long time now people have not been receiving Christian teaching, and there is no background of knowledge about the Christian faith. The regular habit of going to church has been broken now for several generations. Patrick Revell felt that it is going to need some new impact to get the habit started again, and it will require nurture among children. This is going to be difficult while society takes the view that we must be very careful what we teach children – we must not evangelise them and so on. There are not many Church of England schools left – only one or two in the two deaneries in question. Patrick Revell's church had had a visit from a Zambian choir, and the children of the nearby school met them, as they had been doing a project on Zambia. They were amazed to find that the Zambian children's lives were centred on God, something our children had not experienced.

About the traditionalist/renewalist split he said, 'How much better it would be if the old and the new could grow together. We are all part of Christ's body, and no part of Christ's body can say to the other part, "I don't need you – you're old – I don't want you any longer!" ' He was concerned about those who say, 'If the old won't come with us we will have to forget them.' He thought this attitude was too narrow. 'I think you certainly don't want to block the new, I think it is doing wonderful things, but I don't think you should leave people behind. I find it hard to understand those who won't tolerate any new movements at all, and I can't understand those of the new movements who won't have anything to do with the old. I think they are both wrong. I think we both need to grow together.'

He continued, 'I am not sure that these different styles are the key to the whole thing. I think much more the key is experience and knowledge of God. I don't think people understand who or what God is in today's life. Maybe in olden times they did understand that more, and their understanding is not the understanding that we would have today. We are not finding the God of contemporary issues, the God in our lives. It is not related – people are just choosing a hymn

71

that everybody knows, "Praise my soul the king of heaven", for example, but do they know what those words mean? It is superficial, and it is not going to claim people. I have always been puzzled by people's view of the church. There are those of us who love our church life with all its faults, and have a relationship with God – why is it that other people don't see it in that way? Why do we see it in that way? We are no better than they are, we have nothing special.'

Patrick did not know the answer to the problems, but felt that it was important to keep on praying. I reminded him that surveys showed that seventy per cent of people in this country believe in God, and sixty per cent say that they pray sometimes. He replied, 'I don't think it is difficult to believe in God in the sense that there must have been somebody who started all this, but that is totally different from knowing God in your life from day to day, and in particular of course having a Christian faith whereby you relate it to a risen Christ and the guidance of the Holy Spirit.' He felt the need was for lots of Christians to share their faith with other people through the nature of their business, profession, work, friends, marriages. This would get other people to begin to think about God. We need to know our faith and share it with others. The yeast has got to work outside the Church. We talk of the ministry of the laity, but it tends only to happen inside the church building, we need lay ministry in daily life. But people are not missionary-minded enough. Patrick's experience is quite common: 'It was easy to raise £20,000 for the organ – we did it in three months – but if you wanted money for teaching, Bibles, publicity and so on, no way would the money come.'

He is a few years away from retirement, and when he talked to retired clergy they all agreed that they were so glad they were no longer in full-time ministry. They had been able to return to their faith and to their worship, Bible reading and prayer life, and, thank goodness, they no longer had to worry about the Church, they could concentrate on God and their fellow human beings. Patrick Revell concluded, 'We are obsessed with structures and schemes and measurements. I feel that I would like to take hold of my desk and tip the whole jolly lot into the waste-paper basket. It is all too much – quite indigestible, and the average person in our villages is not being helped by them; it is only the spiritual that will help them.'

Patrick Revell is speaking from a traditional background and experience and a church with an average attendance of 160, though it is declining because of the advanced age of those taking part. I have found that those attending traditional churches have difficulty in believing that their church could be renewed because they have no experience of it. On the other hand those in the renewed churches cannot appreciate the depths of the crisis that many traditional churches are in, because in the same way, they have no experience of what it is like to be in a church that is declining or struggling to keep going.

It is interesting to compare what Patrick Revell said with the experience of Bishop David Pytches, of St Andrew's, Chorleywood, who leads a church which has embraced Charismatic renewal from the beginning of the Charismatic movement. In his church people are converted every Sunday, such is the power of the worship of the congregation and the Holy Spirit at work in it. They are best known for their outreach work in teaching and encouragement in the New Wine Christian family conferences which attract around thirteen thousand people each year.

The theme of the conferences for this year (1995) was taken from Isaiah 43:19, 'See, I am doing a new thing! Now it springs up; do you not perceive it? I am making a way in the desert and streams in the wasteland.'

I spoke to David Pytches who explained to me how he sees it: 'God is a living God and he is always doing new things. If we change our attitude and begin to look to the new thing that God is doing, and go with that, God will lead us, which doesn't mean that he will lead us all in the same way, because I don't think God makes clone churches. He will lead us in the ways of righteousness and of life and of faithfulness, but I think we have a mind-set. The mind-set of the Jews in Isaiah's day was that the great thing that God had done was to bring them through the Red Sea, that is, he cut a dry bed through the Sea, and that was the mind-set. But in Isaiah God says, "I am going to do a new thing, I am going to cut a stream through the desert." In other words, it was a complete reversal of what he had done before, and I think we find that we quickly become so traditionalist that we can't fit the new thing God is doing into our focus. If we don't go with the new thing, if we don't bless what God is doing, what is there, because the old is crumbling away? This is why I have such hope because I know that God is a living God and I know he is doing new things. I know God wants to bless his people and really loves his Church. It may mean that we have to let go of some good things, maybe only for a while, and the

Holy Spirit will bring them back in. Gregorian chants came back into vogue last year with young people, because of this monastery in Spain. I feel that we shouldn't fear, that God will lead his stewards to bring out of his treasure things new and old.

'I think it is very exciting, but it does require courage to move with what you believe God is telling you to do. It is painful, but I think you have to do it. Churches have got to look at their agendas. Are we willing for God to do new things – can we resource any new things?

'In St Andrew's we looked at what we were supporting and I said, "Do we have to continue to support all these things?" because when someone came up with a new vision we hadn't any money to do anything about it, because we always seemed committed to so many old things. We need to bless what God is doing. He will then bless us so much more than if we ask him to come and bless us for what we are trying to do. I believe that with all my heart. I have to say that we have seen that happen in a wonderful way. We have seen a full church for a long time (about a thousand, including children, passing through the doors every Sunday), and we have sent people out to get new churches going.

'We are keeping our church within the Anglican fold because I am a child of the Anglican Church, I love the Church of England and I think – why do we have to lose all our people to new denominations, because after a couple of decades all the new churches start to have the problems that all the old churches had. I feel that it is a pity they can't remain within this fellowship of the Church of England, and when you look back at history you can see how

75

flexible the Church of England has been in the past. We must find ways to hold the new within the family of the Church of England. We could have had temptations at one stage to go off and get a really big thing going but we have never wanted to break with the Anglican Church. We have developed instead the New Wine conferences because we felt that that was God's will for us. We run clergy days, and if we can encourage one thousand clergy to go off and do new things, that is far more exciting. When I am dead and gone, whatever is of God will go on, but whatever is of us will join us in the grave.

'Charismatics are accused of being frothy, but St Andrew's must be one of the biggest givers in the diocese (St Albans). Our people seek to read their Bibles and to pray, and are concerned about God's causes in the world. We are not the rich end of Chorleywood, people are giving sacrificially. I see genuine Christians walking deeply with God and tithing their income, there is nothing frothy in that.

'The next step churches need to take is an openness to the Holy Spirit and a recognition of the supernatural dimension of the Kingdom of God. We need to praise God for what he is doing. This doesn't mean throwing away our discernment and not using our brains, but we need to be more humble and recognise that God's thoughts are not our thoughts, his ways are higher than our ways, although he often works with us. So we need to be open to the Holy Spirit and allow him to touch us deeply in our lives.' David Pytches has been observing this amongst his own people and finds it interesting to see how God is leading them. A prophecy given one Sunday was, 'Fill them up and send them out!' The music leader came up with a worship song the following week entitled 'Fill them up and send them out!' God has been sending people out from St Andrew's all over the world. David Pytches said, 'We don't like seeing our good people go, but it is God who is at work in this way, so we believe that he will replace them.'

The new theologians are becoming open to the supernatural. They have seen the old style theologians put God into a box which has become a coffin. It was a theology of despair and destruction, but things are now changing. The Bible carries its own authenticity and is captivating the new generation.

David Pytches believes that we have somehow got to find a way of building the new that does not destroy all the old. 'If we criticise some of the things that are very precious to other people who are more traditional than we are, why are we criticising them? What we are really saying is that we are concerned that those things won't bring in the next generation, but they are nevertheless very meaningful to those who are there. I see a lot of churches, and I have to say, "You mustn't feel guilty that you are unable to move into a more renewed church, somebody has got to look after these people! So I would want to bless that, but you might find that the older people would help you resource a new thing, perhaps in some other premises, for their children and grandchildren. Some of these elderly people might be so excited about that, particularly if they knew you were not going to take away from them some traditional rituals which have become a major support to them over the years in their walk with God."

'Wherever you are in the churchmanship spectrum we are all in the same position. I have radical people that I can't hold, they want to go off to something which is far more liberated than we are in the Church of England. So it doesn't matter where you are, you have always got some people who are more radical, or much more traditionalist than you are as a leader. I think these are very difficult times for our clergy, and some of them have been very hurt by the renewal, because some people have been unwise and insensitive (and I include myself in this) in the way they have tried to put it across. And then of course the way they interpret you or me – they classify you and say, "Well this is what these people think, or do," when it may not be the way in which we see things at all. Many of the clergy were not selected because they were leaders, but because they were godly servant pastors. What the Church desperately needs today is leaders, because the pastor finds it difficult, he bleeds for the people who are hurt by the changes. The leader realises that is the situation, but he says, "If we don't make the change, we won't have the Church to meet the needs of the future." '

This is the dilemma which the faithful remnant have to face and with the help of the Holy Spirit overcome if they are to pass on their faith to the new generation. The Church has been here before. Again and again it has been reduced to the faithful remnant, but God has raised it up again for his glory. In the 1830s people were saying that the Church of England was finished, and would not last for another generation, but it was raised up again as a great missionary Church sending out its messengers across the world. Already you can see this beginning to take place in churches like St Andrew's, Chorleywood.

I think the key issue was the one David Pytches

78

put his finger on – openness to the Holy Spirit. A Non-Stipendiary Minister said to me, 'It's the churches that are open to the Holy Spirit that are growing. Jesus said that we should put new wine into new wineskins because old ones crack and split and leak. The Church is leaking all over the place. These parishes [a group of rural parishes] could be growing, but the people here don't want it, they won't throw away the old wineskins.'

Let David Pytches have the last word: 'The Church needs to change its attitude – it needs to change its mind. It needs to capture a vision of the supernatural – the presence and glory of God. The Church needs to repent that it has lost its vision because God is still here. We also need to repent that we have lost our faith and courage, which is linked to a loss of vision. Once we have seen the light, as it were, we are invincible and press on. This is not necessarily the leaders' fault – we all need to repent, we all need to become holy. We all have to stand for righteousness, some of us would get martyred for it, but that is a time-honoured way of establishing the point. I am sure that we need to repent as a Church and, although I find this difficult, I need to repent of my own moral sins. Part of repentance means mourning and grieving, and I think we all need to grieve over the state of the nation. "Blessed are they that mourn." I feel that I am mourning because the Church seems to have lost its soul. What will remain for my children and grandchildren to inherit of our spiritual riches? Yet I believe there is a way forward, and light at the end of the tunnel.'

Loving God, Father of all,
we come to listen for your voice amidst the
  clamour of this unsettled world.
Give us grace to hear your message; give us
  courage to respond.
Let a fresh breath of heaven blow through your
  Church
to quicken our love for you and for each other.
By the power of your Holy Spirit prepare us to
  spread
the good news of the living gospel, Jesus Christ,
  our beloved Lord and Saviour. Amen.

(Mission Prayer of the Diocese of Bath and Wells.)

Study

BIBLE READING: NEHEMIAH 7

QUESTIONS FOR MEDITATION/DISCUSSION

1. What do you believe God is saying to us through
    the decline and growth that is taking place in the
    Church today?
2. What is God calling you to do and be as part of
    the faithful remnant?
3. What do you believe that God is calling your
    own church to in this situation?

PRAYER

Pray for the Church in England, ending with the
Mission Prayer.

7

The Rediscovery of the Scriptures

Chapter 8 of the book of Nehemiah opens with the people assembled in the square before the Water Gate of Jerusalem. They ask Ezra to bring out the book of the Law and read it to them. The book of Ezra and the book of Nehemiah have been grouped together from earliest times. Tradition has it that Ezra returned to Jerusalem before Nehemiah, but the internal evidence of this chapter is that Ezra and Nehemiah were contemporaries, and were living in Jerusalem at the same time.

Ezra reads the book aloud to the people, who listen attentively. Women and children were not allowed to attend assemblies apart from on exceptional occasions. This seems to have been one of them – all who could understand were allowed to attend. The Levites instruct the people in the Law 'making it clear' or 'translating it'. It is not apparent from the text whether they were giving a commentary on it or translating it for the benefit of those who did not speak Hebrew, but here again the emphasis is on understanding what was read (verse 8).

When they hear the Law, the people weep, presumably because they had not been obeying it, but they are told not to cry but to go and feast with great joy, 'because they now understood the words that had been made known to them' (verse 12). 'Do not grieve,' says Nehemiah, 'for the joy of the Lord is your strength' (verse 10). The people go away to eat and drink, and are told also to give food to those who have nothing prepared.

The next day, as they continue to read the Law, they discover the Feast of Tabernacles was due to be celebrated at that time (the seventh month) so they all build booths from branches of olive trees, myrtles, palms and other trees to live in during the feast.

The people celebrate the feast for seven days with great joy, and on the eighth day there is another assembly, which is reported in the next two chapters.

This is an exciting chapter which reports vividly the stunning effect that the reading of the Law had upon the people. The freshness of rediscovering the Scriptures comes over strongly – they respond in repentance and then great joy, because they have understood God's Word to them.

Today the importance of the Scriptures, and particularly the Old Testament, has been undermined by critical liberal theology. One speaker I heard described this process as being like dismembering an onion to see what it is made of, and being left with nothing but the bits. As a result the authority of the Bible as the Word of God has been undermined, and many church people do not look to it for inspiration and guidance, whilst outside the Church there is now a widespread ignorance of the Bible and what it has to say about God and his relationship to us. The time is ripe for a rediscovery of the Scriptures, Old and New, but particularly of the Old Testament. This is now beginning to take place, partly as a result of spiritual renewal, which brings the Scriptures alive through the inspiration of the Holy Spirit.

I talked about the new approach by scholars to John Bimson, lecturer in Old Testament Studies at Trinity College, Bristol. He told me that there was a rediscovery of Scripture going on in Old Testament Studies – in terms of new ways of reading the text which are not destructive but which look at the text as it stands. Some scholars have now taken the emphasis away from looking primarily at sources and layers of tradition, considering that to be an old-fashioned approach which in the end does not produce any really useful result as far as the Church is concerned. The emphasis now is much more on taking the text as we have it, and employing more sensitive ways of reading it as literature, asking what the message is, what the final shape is.

The Old Testament scholar who has written most about this is Brevard Childs. He has introduced what he calls a canonical approach, which means that Scripture is viewed in its canonical shape. For example, if a person is looking at the book of Amos, instead of asking the old questions (such as, is the second half of chapter 9 original to Amos, or should it be disregarded in order to get back to the original text?), he would say, regardless of any personal opinion about those particular verses, the right way to interpret the book is in its final canonical form. His other emphasis is to take seriously the fact that individual books of Scripture do not come to us as unique books, but as part of a canon, so that they need to be read in relation to each other as well. In the Christian community of faith anyone who is studying the Bible also needs to ask what light a New Testament passage throws on an Old Testament passage, and vice versa. Brevard Childs has been championing this approach since the 1970s.

This is a controversial approach and Brevard Childs' critics have accused him of going back to a pre-critical almost fundamentalist stance. He denies that, and says he is making use of all the tools that criticism provides, but placing the emphasis on why the text is in the shape it is now, and what it has to say. Other scholars are also working with the final form of the text, but without his emphasis on canon.

Walter Brueggemann has written an enormous number of books using this approach, as has John Goldingay. Walter Brueggemann is rediscovering Scripture as revelation. He is keen on Scripture as revelation and as having authority as it speaks today. So within Old Testament circles there is a rediscovery of Scripture's authority, and its power to speak to contemporary situations. This is a radical change from John Bimson's student days in the seventies, when it was very much a dissection of the text. There was a danger of losing sight of the text as a whole, and certainly any message and relevance it might have for the contemporary church, but these new approaches are, from the Church's point of view, user-friendly.

This is now the main trend in Old Testament scholarship at the moment – reading the text in its final form, reading it as narrative, reading it with sensitivity to its literary qualities, placing the emphasis on understanding more clearly all the layers of meaning. Even in Ezra and Nehemiah's day there was a need for the Law and Pentateuch to be applied and explained, because they were no longer living in the same land or culture in which the laws were given and they were no longer a nomadic, pastoral society. The modern problem of bridging the cultural gap between the Bible and contemporary life is in fact a very old one.

John Bimson thinks that in teaching the Old Testament there is a danger of falling into one of two extremes. The first is the tendency to emphasise that it is an ancient piece of literature from a very different culture, with the result that it becomes distant and irrelevant, merely an historical document. The other error is to overlook these factors altogether and read the Bible as if it is immediately relevant to contemporary society, giving the impression that one can open it anywhere and it will have something to say to our situation. Both of these extremes are dangerous. We need what Tony Thistleton (lecturer in Hermeneutics and principal of St John's College, Durham) calls 'distancing and fusion'! Distancing takes account of the 'otherness' of the document, while fusion enables the parallels to come together and click for that moment of revelation. For example, Luther experienced this when he realised the relevance of Paul's teaching of Law and grace to his own culture. There is a 'click' when the two horizons come together. The picture suddenly makes sense.

I asked John Bimson about the Bible as revelation earthed in history and a specific culture – what is cultural and what is for eternity?

John Bimson replied that it is a matter of discovering principles which are abiding, even though the specific situations may not be. Two important examples of this are the Old Testament laws about caring for the poor, not harvesting right to the edges of the fields so that the poor could glean the rest, and the Jubilee Year when debts were cancelled, people could go back to their land, and slaves were set free. They contain principles about the need for any society to care for the poor, and to have some kind of brake on the accumulation of wealth by some at the expense of others. The principles are abiding even though the exact situations no longer exist.

In other words, there is no short cut to studying the Old Testament. In terms of Nehemiah 8 there is still a need for our equivalent of the Levites, the priests, to do the bridging, the interpretation. John Bimson regrets that so many churches have given up on the Old Testament, because it reinforces the impression that this is an old book which has been superseded by the New Testament, and that we do not need to pay much attention to it.

There is another strand in Old Testament scholarship at the moment, namely an extreme scepticism as to the historicity of the Old Testament. So at the same time that many scholars are looking at the text as a whole, and rediscovering it as revelation, authority and canon, other scholars are saying, 'We don't actually believe that any of this happened!' They would not believe that there was an Exodus, or a conquest, or a Judges period. Some do not even accept that the monarchy began in the way in which the Bible says it happened, and they throw doubts on the stories of Saul, David and Solomon. So these two contrasting approaches are going on, on two parallel tracks that never meet. John Goldingay stresses that history and theology in the Old Testa-

ment are inextricably linked together. The claims that
the Old Testament makes about the character of the
God who has done certain things are essential: 'You
can't have the theology if you are going to deny the
historicity.'

John Bimson believes that the historicity is very
important, and agrees with John Goldingay on this
matter. He feels that it is important to discern what
kind of genre we are reading. When he is reading
Exodus, Joshua, Judges, Kings, for example, he
regards it as theologised history, and not history as
we know it in the Western world. In his view it is
important to believe basically that the events happened. He would read Genesis 1 in a different way.
It is metaphorical in style, so although he would
want to say, 'Yes, there was an act of disobedience,
and there certainly was a Fall', he would not want to
insist that it involved a speaking serpent and eating a
piece of fruit. Metaphorical language is being used
here to talk about events that otherwise we cannot
get back to at all.

He takes the view that Nehemiah is fairly straightforward reporting of what happened, but obviously
a selective reporting: the writer is not telling us every
single incident here, but picking out those things
which have theological significance for him. There
are two processes of selection going on. There is the
writer's own process of selection – deciding what is
important to make his point – and then there is the
selection of those who canonised the books, who
decided that this book is important, and there may
also be editorial activity by them. In his opinion it is
what speaks to the community at each stage of the
process that gets preserved. We need to take this

seriously, and to say that the book has achieved this final form because it went through this process. Part of the reason why the final form is important is because the community of faith felt this was the right shape for it, and that it had something important to say to the church. Books were canonised because they were so relevant, and because they had proved their worth to the community.

As a scholar John Bimson thinks that a great deal depends on the presuppositions we bring to the text, and how far we allow the Bible to challenge our presuppositions and reshape them.

He values the new literary approach and takes the view that when we read the Bible we enter a world that is different from our own, and if we are open to it the Bible will challenge our world-view and give us a new world-view that is more realistic because it has got the divine dimension in it, which our world has had squeezed out of it. He thinks that some of the scholars who are extremely sceptical about historicity are actually trying out an idea which they then push to extremes. Some contemporary scholars are trying to prove that various parts of the Bible were written later and later. The most extreme form of this was a paper written last year by a Scandinavian theologian who wants to argue that the entire Old Testament was written in the Hellenistic era after 300 BC. In order to prove something like that it is necessary to prove that the texts are not historical and not based on earlier sources, but that they were written from scratch at that time, and so obviously cannot preserve anything historical about the Exodus, or the patriarchs, for example. In cases like this the theory that is being tested simply takes over and excludes other possibilities. These extremely sceptical views are now held by a minority of biblical scholars. Different approaches tend to do their own thing, and do not have very much dialogue with other groups. So there is really no debate between those who think the text is authoritative and those who say there is no historicity – there is no meeting point.

So the Old Testament is being rediscovered in our day by scholars as revelation, as canon, and as something that has authority today. This means that the theological college has a very important role in trying to break into a vicious circle. If the clergy undervalue the Old Testament, and do not read it or teach it in church or preach on it, the congregation will not know how to read it, and will get the message that it is an irrelevant book. At theological college there is the opportunity to study the Old Testament as an extremely important piece of Scripture.

If a model can be given of how to read the Old Testament, the students when they leave college will pass on this model to their parishes, so strategically Old Testament studies in theological college are very important. What worries John Bimson is that the process is extremely slow. Clergy who were taught in the sixties and the seventies that only the New Testament was important are still operating on that premise, and do not know anything about recent studies. They often look at the new approaches as an Evangelical Trojan horse, whereas in fact the new ways of looking at the Old Testament are much broader than that, and many of the scholars doing this new work are not Evangelical at all.

Another way in which the Scriptures are being

rediscovered is through spiritual renewal. It seems to be a universal experience of all kinds of spiritual renewal that the Holy Spirit brings the Scriptures to life and speaks through them. A clergy friend who experienced spiritual renewal said that before renewal he had always thought of the Old Testament as something he had to wade through to get to the New Testament, but that afterwards God started to speak through the Old Testament as well as through the New.

I spoke to the Revd Preb. Patrick Riley, who comes from a Liberal Catholic background, but who has experienced charismatic renewal, and whose parish is currently being touched by the so-called 'Toronto Blessing', about the rediscovery of the Scriptures after renewal. He finds that the people he serves have a hunger to know what God is going to say to them through the day's reading. If they had not already found God or been found by him, they would not be looking for him in the Scriptures, and if they were not looking for God in the Scriptures they would not be able to find him there. It is a peculiar paradox: we have to be renewed in our heart before we can find God in Scripture. The relationship with God comes first.

He believes that this generation is looking for spiritual experience. He commented, 'Up till now people have been willing to take an analytical and logical approach, and call that a living faith, when perhaps it never actually lived anything, it has only been cerebrally accepted, not totally received in body, mind and spirit. Nowadays that isn't enough; people want to have, quite rightly I think, certainly in Glastonbury they do, they want to have an experiential faith, one they can see working. Before they commit themselves, they want to see that it is worth committing themselves to. Two New Age bods came into one of our Six O'clock Services. I know they weren't Christians, I could see they weren't Christians, they weren't joining in. I said to them, "Is this worrying you? (People falling over and laughing and so on)." They said, "Oh no, no, there is nothing surprising here. This is what we would expect from the Church." Which is fascinating – they came to Glastonbury looking for experience, bumped into the Church and found it. They weren't a bit surprised because that was what they were looking for. They represent a whole generation of people who are looking for experiential evidence rather than brilliant arguments or closely reasoned Bible study. If they are open to experience, they will find it, but they then have to discern what they are looking at.'

What particularly struck Patrick about Nehemiah 8 was that it was a common experience. The whole congregation came to life together. In the very last verse we are told that they listened to the Word of God, celebrated the Feast of Tabernacles together for seven days, and on the eighth day there was an assembly. He commented that if we had Synod waiting upon God for seven days, studying the Bible and praying together, when we came to our business on the eighth day things might be rather different!

Patrick was also interested in the emphasis on understanding the Scriptures in chapter 8. He argues, as C. S. Lewis does, that it is through the power of poetic language that we are able to understand the quality of experiences which we have not had, or perhaps can never have. It enables us to use the factors within our experience so that they become pointers to factors outside our experience. We have been guilty of playing intellectual games with the Bible. St Augustine said that we must obey in order to understand – not 'I want to understand before I commit myself'. As St Paul says, the natural person cannot understand spiritual things. Spiritual things are spiritually discerned. We are at the end of Enlightenment ways of working at things, which assumed that everything could be organised, and therefore understood. It is the difference between revelation and religion. Patrick Riley commented, 'What we have done is to dehydrate revelation into a cerebral religion which is absolutely fatal, because then people will come to church because it is the one place where they don't get challenged, don't get asked anything, and they don't react to anything because there is nothing to react to. We need to restore revelation through the Bible.'

He went on to say, 'If revelation has been reduced in stature to just being religion and rules, you become not only Pharisees at heart, but also your expectation that God should move today is completely denied, therefore you run the risk of denying the work of the Holy Spirit. You can actually commit the sin of saying that black is white, and white is black, and deny the work of God, which is horrendous. In the aftermath of the Enlightenment and Liberal theology, it is ironic that the so-called Liberal theology should have become illiberal, so uptight that it won't accept anything else, the pieces of onion on the floor bit. This approach has run into dry sand. What God is now doing in the Church is water in dry ground, real refreshment to the soul. It is so wonderful to see what is happening beyond the little cerebral games that we are used to playing with religion. When revelation takes over, and we have, as in Nehemiah 8, a hunger for the Scriptures, a hunger for worship, deep worship together, the corporate nature of what is going on, the excitement and the energy, you suddenly realise that it is very close to the heart of God now, as then!'

Collect for Advent 2

Blessed Lord,
who caused all holy Scriptures
to be written for our learning:
help us so to hear them,
to read, mark, learn and inwardly digest them
that, through patience, and the comfort
    of your holy word,
we may embrace and for ever hold fast
    the hope of everlasting life,
which you have given us in our Saviour Jesus
    Christ.
Amen.*

*Taken from *The Alternative Service Book 1980*.

Study

QUESTIONS FOR MEDITATION/DISCUSSION

1. Do you read the Scriptures as:
    (a) literature,
    (b) history,
    (c) revelation?
    In other words, what is it that you are reading?
2. What place do the Scriptures have in your personal life?
3. What place do the Scriptures have in your own church's life?

PRAYER

Pray about what you have received and wish to receive from the Bible as a Christian, concluding with the Collect for Advent 2.

Further Reading

Brueggemann, Walter, *The Prophetic Imagination* (Fortress).
Biblical Perspectives on Evangelism (SPCK).
The Bible Makes Sense (J. Knox).
The Creative Word (Fortress).
Finally Comes The Poet (Fortress).
Speech For Proclamation (Fortress).

Childs, Brevard, *Biblical Theology of the Old and New Testaments* (SCM).

O.T. Theology in the Canonical Context (SCM).

An Introduction to the O.T. of Scripture (SCM).

Goldingay, John, *Models for Interpreting Scripture* (William).

Models for Scripture (William).

Wright, Christopher, J. H., *The Use of the Bible in Social Ethics* (Grove Books).

8

Worship and Repentance

In chapter 9 of the book of Nehemiah the people assemble together, but this time as penitents, fasting and wearing sackcloth and ashes. It is twenty-four days since Ezra read them the Law, and out of their corporate study of Scriptures, out of their rediscovery of the nature of God, and his claims upon them, comes a corporate act of repentance, set in the context of worship. To begin with they are told to, 'Stand up and praise the Lord your God, who is from everlasting to everlasting' (verse 5). They bless him as the Creator of all things, who is above all and is worshipped by the hosts of heaven. Then starting with Abraham and Moses they tell the story of how God made a special relationship with the people of Israel, how he chose and redeemed them. It puts the whole act of repentance into its context: the great eternal God of all things and his goodness to Israel is contrasted with the disobedience and ungratefulness of Israel. Nevertheless God had compassion on Israel, was patient with them even when they rebelled against him, and time after time had mercy on them when they had suffered as the result of their sin. So in accordance with his revealed love and compassion towards Israel, the people ask him to deliver them from the hardship that has come upon them for they are slaves in the land that God had given them, and they ask him to have mercy on them in their great distress.

The people spend three hours reading the book of the Law, and three hours confessing and worshipping the Lord. This was not an everyday event, but a special occasion, when they wanted to find out what God was saying to them, what the way forward was in a very bleak situation.

They were the faithful remnant starting again in Israel and it was a sacrificial step to take: it was hard to come back and start again in such harsh conditions. I discussed this with Richard Salmon, vicar of Congresbury, and he commented, 'When you've made a sacrifice, and come back, it is easy to feel sorry for yourself and think that the great sacrifice excuses little sins. They may have thought that it didn't matter if they took wives from around about, "We are the faithful remnant, we are here." It is easy after a long time of waiting, for temptation to set in.'

He was very struck by the verse introducing the worship: 'Stand up and praise the Lord your God who is from everlasting to everlasting.' While God's context is from everlasting to everlasting, our context is our limited view of life. God enables us to look at our lives from the viewpoint of eternity, because he wants us to be fit for eternity. Richard said, 'I feel very much that we are being reminded that God is not the invention of our generation, and therefore we can't twist the situation and talk about the nature of the problems of our generation as if it were to change the nature of God. We are still dealing with the eternal God, who became flesh and dwelt among us. That is why we need to worship, and in that light we begin to see that what we are doing is really wrong, because it is just a response to our situation here, and it is actually an affront to the eternal God.' He felt that the confession in the *Book of Common Prayer*'s Communion Service spelt out the objective reality of our affront to God, whereas the modern *Alternative Service Book* confessions were much more about what we have done, and the admission that we are sorry, but that there was no recognition that our sin is an affront to the majesty of God. He said, 'It seems to me that we are much more subjective, whereas what they are doing in the book of Nehemiah is being more objective. They are looking at the reality of God first, and seeing their sin from his point of view, not just from theirs.

'Obviously this is what the worship and the praise were about, and also the way in which they go right back to the beginning, to the great Creator and the great Redeemer. Just as God has organised everything in his amazing wisdom so that the world is available for us to live in now, and because he has done it to bring it to this level, he is not going to be thwarted in accomplishing his purposes. Equally, just as he made his covenant promises to Abraham and his successors, so he was not going to be thwarted in his covenant purposes of redemption. Often when everything looks black and there is no easy way out, we are called just to constant obedience because of the nature of God. It isn't easy.'

Richard Salmon was reminded of the selfishness of our own age, and our unwillingness to settle for God's eternal plan. Our unbelief and hardness of heart towards God have led to disobedience. We have sidelined the resurrection – God's amazing plan – and have concentrated on making a nice place on earth, being swept along with the spirit of the age.

We have tended to write off miracles such as the Virgin Birth and the resurrection, and have forgotten that living a Christlike life is supernatural – if we do not realise this we just go back to what we can cope with, which takes no account of grace. Lowered standards become the norm, because we have dismissed the supernatural element which enables God's standards to be lived out in practice. Just because Christians have sinned, it does not mean that sin is all right: it means that we should seek more earnestly the grace of God's forgiveness, and the grace of transformation. That transformation is not a natural thing but a gift of God, a supernatural gift. Richard said, 'When I think that I can cope with this on my own, then I am in danger, and I fall.'

Anna Tambling, a lay reader, felt that this chapter in Nehemiah was important because it shows us the correct way and order in which things ought to be done. They read the Law first to find out what God wanted of them, and then made a corporate act of worship and confession, all interwoven. She felt that the Church today is out of balance: we don't see the relationship between reading the Word, repentance and worship. We tend to see them all as separate things. She thinks we are bad as a Church at going back to what Scripture says about being the Church – we think we know. We are almost satisfied with the Church as it is, with all its divisions, and we want our own way within it. Both attitudes must cause God terrible pain. Unless we go back to Scripture we will have as many ideas as there are people about what we should be doing and being. When the people of Israel are brought, in this chapter of the book of Nehemiah, to repentance they are also brought back to what their forefathers have done. Anna believes that God is calling us to look at how we have got to where we are and to repent of the failures of the past as well as for the mistakes we are making now. We tend to see repentance as an individual thing. Individual repentance should take place in our private prayer life, but Anna feels that when we come to public worship we should confess our corporate sins as a Church. The Church needs to repent because of what the Church has done. Corporate repentance also includes the sins of our ancestors.

Anna summed up the three areas where she feels we need to repent as a Church:

1. Our acceptance of the divisions, which she feels are scandalous to God.

2. Our refusal to allow Jesus to be the real Head of the Church rather than only a titular one. We behave rather like the servants in the vineyard when their master was away, only in a well-meaning way – we do our best but we don't really seek his will (although he is alive and well and with us by his Holy Spirit).

J. John, the evangelist, tells a story of how he was asked to come and speak to a PCC meeting. He was allowed half an hour on the agenda. When he went along, he found that they had not prayed about the meeting, either before or during it, so he suggested that they should spend the half hour allotted to him, in prayer. They spent eight minutes of the precious half an hour wrangling as to whether they should pray or not, so in the end in despair he said, 'Unless you pray, I am going home, there is no point in having a meeting unless you pray.' J. John says, 'As soon as they had prayed it was obvious what God wanted them to do.' This is where many churches have got to – they feel they must not waste time praying!

Anna told me that she was grieved beyond measure by attending clergy study days, to see such hardworking clergy, who gave so much of themselves, wearing themselves out on *their* schemes, *their* plans for *their* churches and *their* ministry. She said, 'It really grieves me to hear them talking. They are working harder and harder in ever decreasing circles.' She longed to see them accepting what it means to have Jesus as Lord of the Church. It is *his* Church, and it is *his* plans and *his* ministry that they are called to serve; recognising that would lift the burden from their backs through the ministry of the Holy Spirit. Jesus said, 'Take my yoke upon you and learn from me, for I am gentle and humble in heart, and you will find rest for your souls. For my yoke is easy and my burden is light' (Matthew 11:29–30).

3. The third thing we need to repent of is our self-centred approach to the Church – too often we take the approach that the Church is there to please people, whereas it is there to please God. Anna feels, we are all guilty in this regard. She believes the Holy Spirit is saying to us, 'You are all looking for a worship that pleases you; it is only when you are looking for worship that pleases God that you will find unity.'

This she feels is true for all churches, whether young or old, traditionalist or renewed. We all need to find what pleases God. Anna said, 'The word "smugness" comes into mind, there is a satisfaction with the rightness of what the Church is doing even though there is concern that things are not going better. There is no looking at the root of the trouble and asking ourselves are we, his Church, doing what God wants?' The only way to find out what that is, is to read his Word, and listen to his voice. If we do not let the Spirit interpret the Word for us, again we shall have as many interpretations as there are people, but the Spirit speaks in us and through us if we read the Word prayerfully under the Spirit's guidance. Nehemiah 9:20 says, 'You gave your good Spirit to instruct them.' We also need to study the Word together as a church. The church should meet weekly to do this. 'Any live church will naturally do this. In a dead church they can't see why,' Anna said, 'but it is part of being a church, feeding on his Word. It is enrichment, not a daunting study.'

How do we know what pleases God? Anna said, 'I believe that you can know, but only if you wait on him, and only if you ask the Spirit to direct you when you are reading the Word. Even then you have to be continually on your guard against bringing in the bees in your bonnet. You have to pray this away before you can hear what God is saying. It is a case of being constantly purified and coming back to what God wants.'

So unbelief, disobedience and self-centredness are leading us away from God, as they did the Israelites, but there is, I think, a peculiarly English sin, that of well-meaningness. So much of what is done in the Church is done for the best of intentions, but it is our agenda, not God's. Anna said, 'If I thought we

102

were the faithful remnant I would rejoice, because God would be able to use us, but I fear we're the well-meaning remnant.'

Richard Salmon agreed with that because we still have our mind-set blinkered by looking after our church buildings, keeping our structures going, trying to keep the Church of England on the road. We have not allowed God to renew our minds sufficiently, to see ourselves as his people here for this situation. God wants to bless England through his Church.

Being well-meaning is not enough: we need to be an obedient tool in God's hands; instead we are, as the Partners-in-Mission Consultation of 1981 said, 'a rebellious house'.

This brings us under God's judgement, which as Scripture shows is a serious matter we cannot avoid. Anna Tambling was reminded of Romans 11:20–1: 'Do not be arrogant, but be afraid. For if God did not spare the natural branches [Israel], he will not spare you either.' Some people think that the crisis which the Church is undergoing at the moment, particularly the matter of finance in the Church of England, is evidence of God's judgement. He works through crisis, and each crisis is shaking the Church, challenging the very existence of some congregations. Going around the country, I find that some churches are in deep crisis, and have great difficulty in imagining that they could ever be renewed. Others, who are renewed, have difficulty in appreciating just how deep the crisis is that the Church of England faces as a body today.

The book of Nehemiah shows us the way back, which is by corporate worship, repentance and com-

mitment. It demonstrates for us the pattern of under-
taking an act of corporate repentance, following the
pattern of the book of Nehemiah, and this is particularly evident in chapter 9. If you felt this were appropriate in your own church situation, perhaps you
could say together something like this:

Leader: Stand up and praise the Lord your God,
who is from everlasting to everlasting.

(All stand)

All: Blessed be your glorious name, and may
it be exalted above all blessing and praise.
You alone are the Lord. You made the
heavens, and all their starry host, the
earth and all that is in it; the seas and all
the multitudes of heaven worship you.

Leader: Praise the Lord for your creation.

All: May your name be praised for evermore.

Leader: You chose Israel to be your people. You
called Abraham, the man of faith, so that
through him all the people of the earth
should be blessed. You revealed yourself
to him and his descendants and made a
covenant with them. When they suffered
slavery in Egypt, you brought them out
and spoke to them through Moses,
making your will known to them through
your laws.

Leader: Praise you, Lord, for your redemption.

All: May your name be praised for evermore.

Leader: But your people Israel became arrogant
and disobedient. They rebelled against
you, but in your great love you did not
desert them, but brought them safely

through the wilderness into the Promised Land.

All: You gave them the Promised Land, but still they disobeyed you. You sent them your prophets to call them back to you, still they did not listen. You sent them into exile, and they became slaves. They called to you in their misery, and in your great love you heard them and brought them back to the Promised Land.

Leader: Praise you, Lord, sustainer of all life.

All: May your name be praised for evermore.

Leader: In due time you sent us your Son, Jesus.

All: He was born of the Virgin Mary, anointed by the Holy Spirit, and by his life and ministry showed us the Father and himself to be the Way, the Truth and the Life. He was rejected by his own people but to those who believed he gave eternal life. He overcame our sins on the cross, defeated the power of evil, and overcame death by his mighty resurrection. He sent his Holy Spirit on his disciples and raised up a new people of God to glorify his name.

Leader: Praise you, Lord, that you became flesh and dwelt amongst us.

All: May your name be praised for evermore.

Leader: Through his Church missionaries were sent throughout the world.

All: The Christian faith was brought to this country by many missionaries, it took root and filled the land. You raised up a great Church through which this became a Christian country but your Church became greedy and self-seeking, the people disillusioned, and both lost their way. Nevertheless you brought them back to you, renewed and revived your Church, and opened the Scriptures afresh for the building up of your people. Again and again your people have rebelled against you, have lost their faith and deserted you, and again and again in your constant love you have brought them back to you, restored your Church and glorified your name. You raised up a great missionary Church which sent missionaries all over the world.

Leader: Praise you, Lord, for your constant love and forgiveness.

All: May your name be praised for evermore.

Leader: Heavenly Father, for your name's sake and in your love for your Son and for his Church, have mercy on us now for we have been brought low through sin and unbelief.

All: Forgive us, Lord, for your Church has been reduced to a small remnant, and this land can no longer be called a Christian country. Most young people have not heard your gospel and do not know your laws. Have mercy upon your Church, and upon this whole country. In your faithful love and mercy raise up your Church once again so that through it you can bless the whole nation. Help us, your people, to live in love and the freedom of the gospel so that we can witness to your power among us today.

Leader: Praise you, Father, for sending us your Son and your Holy Spirit.

All: May your name be praised for evermore.
Leader: Praise you, Jesus, great Shepherd of the sheep.
All: May your name be praised for evermore.
Leader: Praise you, Holy Spirit, for giving us yourself to lead and guide.
Together: Glory be to the Father, and to the Son, and to the Holy Spirit; as it was in the beginning, is now, and shall be forever. Amen.

A Personal Prayer

O Lord Almighty, Creator and Restorer of all things and all people, I bring before you your Church – formed by you to carry out your will.

Down the ages human beings have divided and torn your Church apart, but you are a God of compassion; we have treated your Church as if it belonged to us, and yet you are a God of mercy.

O Lord, I pray that we, your Church, may be brought to repentance so that we may come before you with deep sorrow and turn back to you in obedience.

We ask this in Jesus' name and for his glory. Amen.

Study

BIBLE READING: NEHEMIAH 9

QUESTIONS FOR MEDITATION/DISCUSSION

1. What does Nehemiah 9 tell us about communal repentance?
2. What particular things do you think your own church has to praise and thank God for? (Use wallchart.)
3. What particular things do you think your own church needs to repent of?

PRAYER

Either with extempore prayer, or using the form of worship and repentance given in this chapter, make a corporate or personal act of worship and repentance.

9

Commitment and Celebration

After the time of worship and repentance, the people of Israel make a binding agreement, which is put in writing, and sealed by the Levites, priests and leaders of the community (eighty-four names in all). They commit themselves to keep the Law of God as given through Moses. In Chapter 10 there is a short passage naming particular laws which they apparently thought it necessary to spell out, presumably because these laws had not been obeyed in the recent past. They concern marriage to foreigners, keeping the Sabbath holy, but particularly the support of the temple life and worship through the offerings that the people were required to give. The chapter ends, 'We will not neglect the house of our God.'

The statement expresses what the people of Israel felt at that time it was necessary for them to do in order to be the people of God fully. We in the Church today are the people of God. What do we need to be committed to in order to be the faithful remnant, the people of God in this nation?

Richard Salmon showed me a copy of a declaration St Andrew's Church, Congresbury had drawn up to express what they believed they were about and should be committed to as a church. It said:

This church is part of the world-wide family of God, called by the Father, cleansed by the Son, set apart for obedience to God by the Holy Spirit to glorify him and to display his life, love and power as a fellowship.

1. We find our security in the love of the Father.
2. We acknowledge Jesus as our Lord and Saviour.
3. We welcome the Holy Spirit and expect to witness his awesome power.
4. We find our fulfilment in obeying God's Word.
5. We pray together as well as individually.
6. We affirm, encourage and support one another in love.
7. We are witnesses to Jesus wherever we go.

Different churches might have different emphases depending on their theology and ecclesiology, but on one thing they would all agree: they are all called to be the people of God in the place and community within which they are set.

Richard Salmon put it like this: 'I believe that God is calling us to be the people of God in this place. It is possible to go off and set up a church where you are able to do all the things that you want to, and see all the blessings, and that's grand, but the fact remains that this village of Congresbury would not be blessed, because if you go off and have a great time somewhere else the village itself loses out. If God is asking us to go on trusting him, that means I want to stick around until he answers. If he has promised blessing, we must stick it out until it comes. OK, it's important to do what the Israelites did and say, "Can we discern any reason why it hasn't happened yet?" This is where the importance of getting together as a congregation comes. It comes out of a corporate reflection, and a corporate study of the Scriptures. It is a very interesting thing, because people are so reluctant to get up and say anything. How can one best provide the environment for this sort of thing to happen? I suppose it ought to be the Annual Church Meeting, when we get together and praise God and wait on him and read his Word. Or perhaps it should be a Quinquennial. Maybe annually is too often, but perhaps every five years all of us should get together to read the Scriptures in groups and discuss what God is saying to us and ask the question, "Are we willing to do it?" '

Richard has been struck by what it says in Revelation 21 about God being at home with his people: 'Now the dwelling of God is with men, and he will live with them. They will be his people, and God himself will be with them and be their God' (verse 3). He believes that we become God's people when we live as if we know that God is at home among us. Some people are great on principles. It is good to have principles, but we are asked to worship the Trinity, a company relating to each other. As we worship the Trinity, we are drawn into their circle. Our worship is God-centred, Person-centred, people-centred, all to do with relationship. The revelation we have in Scripture enables us to see the nature of the God to whom we are relating. This is of great value because we must relate to him in truth, otherwise we change the standard. When we are relating truly to God, we are being this community where he is at home.

God is the Creator, he is the one who has put us here to look after the world, to till it and keep it. Therefore we have this responsibility, and it is right that we should work, but he is also the God who loves us, and therefore we are called to be a community of love. One of the things that James says in his letter is, 'Pray for one another' (5:16). We pray for all sorts of things, but what does the Bible tell us to pray for? Jesus prayed for those who believe, and he taught us to pray for the Kingdom to come. Our failure to pray enough for each other is, Richard thinks, linked to the low level of behaviour in society. By praying for the Church we are praying for the most effective way of helping society. If the Church is holy and obedient, and embodies this life in which people are given their true value, then society will start to change because we are putting Christianity into practice.

We become truly the faithful remnant, and the means through which God can bless our local community, and on a national level, this nation.

Richard felt that in the Church of England the way we view being the Church for the nation is that we should compromise with everything and everyone so that we can try and be accepted in as many circles as we can. We cannot, it seems to him, be a faithful remnant, until we put faith as a significant feature in our Church membership. He said, 'I don't know quite how to do this, but while we don't have any concept of affirmation of faith for electoral roll membership, I don't think we can begin to be a faithful remnant. There is an optional scheme in which, when we have the renewal of the electoral roll, we have an expression of faith which we ask people to sign if they will. We can't force them to do it, so we have a segment of our electoral roll that won't sign it because they don't appear to put the faith as a priority.'

Richard believes that as a Church we should be committed to faith and obedience, and a willingness to be God's people, focusing on God's purposes and being an honour to him, not insisting on getting our own way, or having a comfy time.

If we wish to emulate the Israelites and make our own commitment as a church, we could follow the act of worship and repentance in the previous chapter with a declaration in these or similar words:

All: We are the people of God. He has called and chosen us to serve him in love and obedience. So that through us our society will be blessed. We therefore commit ourselves to the following:

1. To love God and each other in the light of the gospel, being salt and light in our community and a blessing to our neighbours.
2. To acknowledge Jesus as Lord not only with our lips but with our lives, not taking any decisions without prayerfully seeking his will.
3. To allow the Holy Spirit to lead and guide us, and to fill us with his love, peace and joy until we overflow to others.
4. To be good stewards of all God's gifts to us, giving generously to those in need, and fully supporting the work of the Church.
5. As a church to obey Jesus' commands and in his name to preach and teach the gospel of the

Kingdom and the forgiveness of sins, to make disciples, to heal the sick and overcome the power of evil so that his Kingdom may come on earth as it is in heaven.

6. To pray and study the Word of God, both as individuals and as a church, so that we may hold the faith of Jesus Christ through good times and bad to the glory of his name.

All: May God give us grace to hold fast to this commitment and glorify him for ever.

The Israelites follow their expression of commitment with a special act of celebration to thank God for the rebuilding of the wall of Jerusalem. First there is a purification of the priests and Levites, and then the people, followed by the gates and the wall. The people then split into groups led by choirs and their leaders and march along the top of the wall, but in opposite directions.

They sing and play as they march and after circumnavigating the walls, both groups take their places in the temple, offering sacrifices with great joy. The women and the children also rejoice, and we are told that the sound of rejoicing could be heard far away.

We cannot rejoice because the walls have been rebuilt, because the task has only just begun to happen, but we can rejoice and celebrate Jesus, because he is unchanging love, and he is alive and with his Church as we assemble together. We talk about celebrating Easter and Christmas, and celebrating the Eucharist – but are they joyful celebra-

tions like those described in Nehemiah 12:27–43? I
find that many churchgoers do not know that the
word 'Eucharist' means thanksgiving, and many so-
called celebrations are sombre and routine. Yet we
only need the gentlest touch of the Holy Spirit, the
softest brush of the dove's wing, in order to want to
worship, praise and thank Jesus for his life, death
and resurrection. In the Church of England we are,
I think, better at celebrating than we were, but we
still have a long way to go if we are to celebrate so
exuberantly that the whole neighbourhood is aware
of our great joy! I spoke to Patrick Revell, who said,
'We must get some more rejoicing going alongside a
bleak world.'

Some time ago I was in a service at Holy Trinity
Brompton, when I met an American lady who was
working over here and had wandered into the
service not knowing what to expect. Afterwards she
said to me, 'At home we go to church because it is
the thing to do, but these people are here because
they want to worship God. They were crying and
laughing and dancing! Is that the Church of
England?!' Well it is the Church of England, but not
I fear typical of it, though it is characteristic of those
parishes which have experienced renewal.

Of the parishes that have experienced renewal
known to me personally, the one that emphasises
celebration most strongly is St Andrew's, Chorleywood. At the conferences they hold, each day of
seminars ends with a time of celebration every evening. Bishop David Pytches told me that his people
enjoy celebration most; they love to celebrate. He
and his team encourage people to tell God from their
heart that they love him. They do not talk about God

very much, they address him directly and tell him that they love him. They are trying to bless God. David Pytches said, 'We bless God, and as we bless him, he blesses us; he builds us up, and he sends us out with new faith, new hope, new love, and new vision. At the same time he releases his gifts to his people. When we bless God for his glory he gives it to us. It is very intimate, it strips away our masks, and at the end the whole congregation is on the same level. The celebration is the climax of our relationship with God. It is something we look forward to, we love it.'

In my own diocese of Bath and Wells, the Diocesan Renewal Group holds a six-week course of teaching in five different venues in the diocese. On the seventh week we all come together in Wells Cathedral and hold an Advent Rally of Praise which is an evening of celebration. It is always moving to see the cathedral packed with people praising God. Two years ago, as I led the congregation in prayer, I saw with my spiritual eyes a picture of a group of monks dressed in brown habits who were worshipping with us, and who seemed to be rooting for us. I was encouraged to share this picture with the congregation, and afterwards a couple came up and spoke to me. They had undertaken some research into the history of the cathedral, and had discovered that it had been founded as a missionary centre in Anglo-Saxon times, by a group of monks who met together for worship in the mornings, and in the afternoons went out in boats, since the area was more watery than it is now, evangelising the villages around. Maybe it was those monks, now part of the communion of saints, who were worshipping with us.

Whether that was so or not, we need such missionaries in all our churches today. I believe that it is only as we come together to celebrate God's great goodness, love and power, and to bless him and tell him that we love him, that we will be built up, as David Pytches said, in faith, love and hope, and be strengthened to go out and share our faith with others.

Psalm 100

Cry out with joy to the Lord, all the earth.
Serve the Lord with gladness.
Come before him, singing with joy.

Know that he, the Lord, is God.
He made us, we belong to him,
we are his people, the sheep of his flock.

Go within his gates, giving thanks.
Enter his courts with songs of praise.
Give thanks to him and bless his name.

Indeed, how good is the Lord,
eternal his merciful love.
He is faithful from age to age.

(Mary Calvert*)

*Taken from *The Psalms: A New Translation* published by Harper-Collins Ltd.

Study

BIBLE READING: NEHEMIAH 10 AND 12:27–END

QUESTIONS FOR MEDITATION / DISCUSSION

1. What do the readings tell us about:
    (a) commitment,
    (b) celebration?
2. What particular things do you think your own church should be committed to? (Use wallchart.)
3. Is your church good at celebrating? If not, what would you like to see happening? What have you got to celebrate?

PRAYER

Make a corporate or personal act of commitment, either extempore or using the given form included in this chapter. End with a time of celebration, using Psalm 100.

10

Discipline and Perseverance

The book of Nehemiah does not end, as it might have done, on a high note of celebration with the Israelites processing in triumph around the rebuilt walls of Jerusalem. Instead we come down to earth with a bump. Nehemiah comes back from a visit to Babylon to find that while the cat has been away, the mice have been up to mischief. Without having any authority to do so, Tobiah has been allowed to store his furniture in the consecrated rooms of the temple, which should have been storing the tithes. The rooms are not storing the tithes because the people, contrary to the solemn commitment they have given, have not been bringing the tithes to the temple. Because the tithes have not been coming in, the Levites and the singers have deserted their temple posts and gone to till their own fields. There have also been abuses of the Sabbath day, with people working and trading although this was expressly forbidden by the Law of Moses. Marriages to foreigners have also taken place, with the result that some of the children cannot speak Hebrew.

Nehemiah deals with all this wrongdoing sternly and expeditiously. We see him in this chapter as a leader who is not afraid to be a disciplinarian. He brings his people up to the mark, and insists on them persevering with their commitment to the Law of Moses.

J. John, the evangelist, gave an excellent series of talks on leadership, based on the book of Nehemiah.* He pointed out that Nehemiah exhibits two types of leadership. The first is that of the catalyst: he gets things going, he is the designer, the motivator, the entrepreneur. Chapters 1–6 show him in this role, but as the project grows and changes from rebuilding the walls to building and maintaining the city, his function changes. He becomes the consolidator who has to keep things going, to develop, to manage. It becomes an executive role. In chapters 7–13 we see him exercising this role. Most leaders are either catalysts or consolidators; it is rare to find someone like Nehemiah who has both sets of skills. As an entrepreneur he needed to be involved in everything, but as the project grows, more leaders are needed and so we see him recruiting leaders, delegating responsibility to them, and recording progress. He chooses leaders who have been tested on their personal life for integrity, godliness and faithfulness, and also on past performance. He records three complete lists of people involved in the repopulation and work of rebuilding. He also has to raise financial support. Nehemiah makes the greatest contribution and other leaders also set an example, but everyone gives what they can. Then, in the final chapter, we see him bring-

*Available on tape from The Philo Trust, 91 Woodbank Drive, Wollaton, Nottingham, NG8 2QW. Tel: 0115 9282162; Fax: 0115 9854142.

ing the people back to order, to first principles and to continuing what they have begun.

Chapter 10 gives us a very necessary dose of reality. It is in the everyday, nitty-gritty of following Jesus that things are accomplished for the Kingdom, not in the high moments, though we need those to encourage us. Jesus calls us to be disciples, and that means discipline and perseverance in following him and living according to the will of God the Father as he did on earth. So chapter 10 is 'where it is at' for most of us Christians, most of the time.

I talked to two clergy who were concerned with establishing church plants. The Revd Adrian Hallett was involved in a church plant in his village of Stoke-sub-Hamdon. The new church was planted three years ago as the result of steady growth in the mother church, St Mary's, which had led to an increase of numbers and the need to overflow. Growth had come through house groups and a discipleship course, and the fact that they were still growing steadily meant they were ready to plant. St Mary's is at the eastern end of the village, and the new church was planted at the western end in the village hall.

The motives behind the enthusiasm to plant quickly came to the fore. People agreed with Adrian's vision for setting up the new church: it was to be a church for the unchurched, a frontline mission post reaching out to the people without a church background. It soon became clear, however, that motives were mixed and some people felt, 'This is great, we have our own church now and we can do our own thing, go our own way.' Adrian began to feel uneasy about this, and his apprehension grew

121

when the new church became a cosy club for those who liked that sort of thing, as they settled into becoming a church for themselves. The nucleus of the church plant comprised ex-chapel people and people with a house church background, who were not strong Anglicans, and the new church was more like what they were used to. But as a result of the increasing inward-lookingness, growth has plateaued out, and it is beginning to lose the regular commitment of its members. Both the mother church and the planted church have lost commitment.

When Adrian came back from his sabbatical he felt that the Lord was showing him that the churches needed to come back together again for a period of time to be strengthened. He felt that God was speaking to them through Revelation 3:2: 'Wake up! Strengthen what remains and is about to die'. This seemed to be a warning that not only decline but death was in the offing, so the decision was made to come back together in the autumn of 1995. Adrian feels that there is now a need for in-depth teaching because of confusion over what is happening in the wider Church, and also the impact of the New Age movement. He wants to give some solid teaching to enable the church to grow – meat instead of milk. He sees this as a tactical retrenchment, a time of pruning because motivation has not been right. The whole spirit of the church needs to be restored and put right. Adrian believes that God has been speaking to them through Ezekiel 17 about doing things in their own strength. He thinks that in planting the church they were acting out of enthusiasm, and that there is a need for purification so that the church will grow again in a healthy way. They put a lot of effort into the new church, and there has been bitter disappointment at the decision, but the majority sensed that something radical needed to be done.

So a time of pruning is needed so that the new growth will be healthy and vigorous. This church is learning from its mistakes and realises it will have to take the next step on the Lord's terms, not their own. Vision and strategy are not enough, there is a need for constant navigation to find the way forward. For example, their experience was that people became so involved with the church that eventually they dried up through constant activity. The decision has, therefore, been made to cut down on the number of things going on, although they are running an Alpha course in the autumn. Constant fine-tuning is necessary – people need to receive as well as give. Eternal vigilance is the price of freedom, and this means that there always needs to be a hand on the tiller.

The need for perseverance and discipline is an unpopular message for people today – everything must happen 'now'. It is a constant battle to get people to learn this. Young people in particular have difficulty in recognising that a characteristic of the Christian life is perseverance. It has negative overtones for people today, but it is a great biblical theme. Churches can fall into the trap of trying to meet the instant needs that people have, and to enable them to live on a spiritual 'high'. They can achieve this for so long, but eventually people have to come down into the real world and plod on.

Adrian Hallett feels that an essential aspect of the Christian life is being able to carry on, to persevere. William Carey, the missionary, said to a nephew, 'If people decide to write anything about me after I have gone, say that I can plod. The one thing I have been able to do is to keep going.' Adrian feels that this attitude is so different from what is happening today. He commented, 'People start things but do not see them through, they have vision and enthusiasm, but when they get into the daily grind, the nitty-gritty, and realise the cost of it, it just fizzles. We have got to start building our people and making them disciples. Not people who come to church for entertainment, not to be comfortable, but actually to make them disciples. That is not going to be popular with some, because there is always a cost, but I think nevertheless we have got to build them up and make disciples of them, because that is what we are called to do. We are trying to make things easy for people, whereas discipleship is costly. If people are filled with the Spirit, and go out, they are going to meet with opposition. We don't seem to be preparing our people for that, and because they are not prepared, when the opposition does come, they are not able to deal with it.'

Adrian and I agree that the Church of England is having trouble over discipline, and because of this has been shooting herself in the foot. We have muddled up the need for discipline and the need for pastoral care. We all fail, and we all sin, but God has given us standards to live by. There is always a way back and a fresh start, for those who have failed, but that is meaningless unless we have standards and discipline.

One of the hardest matters of discipline that Anglican clergy have to tackle is the baptism of babies whose parents would never otherwise darken the door of the Church. In spite of strenuous efforts to explain the solemn commitments to God that the parents and godparents make in baptism, and the fact that parents are asking for church membership for their babies, nevertheless many of these people never come back to church again, or bring their children to Sunday School. This leads one to question whether they have understood and believed anything that they have committed themselves to. Richard Salmon told me about one family whose baby's baptism had been included in the morning service so as to enable the congregation to welcome them into the family of the church; the family had walked out in the middle of the service once their baptism bit had been done.

Each clergyman that I talked to had a different approach to the question. Patrick Revell, the most traditional, saw no problem in baptising on demand, and thought there should be no rules about it. But the clergy in the renewal constituency were more concerned about what to do. Patrick Riley commented that under Canon Law baptism could not be refused, but said that he tried hard to explain to non-church members what it entailed, the parents received an invitation to an Alpha course, which has an excellent record of conversions, and they all had a follow-up visit. Captain Phil Baines, who runs a church plant in Nailsea, said that he did not pull out people's hair as Nehemiah did but he pulled out his own in despair at this vexed question! He added that recently in their church they have begun to offer non-church members a thanksgiving for the birth of their baby, which did not involve them in any commitment, but they invited those who on reflection felt able to make the commitment to come back again for the baptism of their baby. He felt that this policy enabled them to get alongside people better.

The figures for the Church of England show that the number of babies being baptised is decreasing, but that the number of adult baptisms is on the increase, so the Church of England generally seems to be going for adult conversion rather than the nominal baptism of babies. This is a hopeful sign, because the work that has been done on church growth, both in this country and in the United States, shows that the more that is demanded of people, the more they give, whereas to demand little leads to decline. In his book *Leading Your Church to Growth** Peter Wagner shows that churches can be placed on a sliding scale depending on how much they ask of their adherents. The more they ask, the more missionary they are, the more they will grow, but they will become more sectarian in nature. This tendency can be seen in the growing churches in this country, and raises a problem for the Church of England, which does not see itself as being sectarian, but as a Church for the nation. State Churches all over Western Europe are in decline, however, and Peter Wagner's book offers an explanation as to why this may be. I recommend this book to all who are concerned about their church policy, whether concerning baptism or other issues, but their baptism policy will accurately indicate where they can be placed on the sliding scale.

Another church plant that shows vividly both the rewards and difficulties of mission in this country is the Trendlewood church plant, an offshoot of Holy

*Published by MARC Europe, 1986.

Trinity, Nailsea, which is presently run by the Church Army Captain, Phil Baines.

The Trendlewood estate was built during the late seventies and early eighties, and is still being added to. The residents mostly commute to Bristol, and are a very mobile population, leading to a high turnover in housing and church attendance. During the recession there have been some redundancies, which have caused anxiety.

The church plant started in a local pub. There are very few meeting places on the estate, and the leisure centre was too expensive to hire. The pub was a good place to start, being a natural meeting place for many people, and the church grew quickly from ten couples to about eighty people, until there was no more room at the inn. They moved to the local Roman Catholic Primary School, where they were made welcome. They continued to grow, and peaked at around one hundred and fifty to two hundred people. Now six and a half years on about one hundred and twenty people belong.

Phil Baines explained the rise and decline of growth: to begin with the church was new and out-ward-looking and it had a bubbly freshness, but, as in Stoke-sub-Hamdon, the more settled church tended to look inwards rather than outwards. They are now trying to redress the balance. As their people mature in faith the emphasis has been on taking faith to be lived out in their place of work, in their famil-ies, and among their friends, rather than bringing people into church.

The church consists mostly of young families (the teenagers attend evening services at Holy Trinity), and the worship is modern, with worship songs.

They have a monthly communion service and a monthly family service, otherwise the children split off for teaching, and meet with the adults for worship at the end. Newcomers can be put off by not knowing the songs, and the charismatic style of worship is difficult for some. Phil tries to explain what is happening for newcomers. Occasionally they run guest services, and invite testimonies from church members. On Christmas Eve, they go back to the pub where the church was born and sing carols.

In their contact with the rest of the estate they find that people are seeking some kind of spirituality, but they tend to have a pick-and-mix approach. They want to be in charge, rather than to submit their lives under Christ's Lordship.

Older people sometimes look to the church for help, but younger people do not. There is difficulty in making relationships with neighbours, because people lead very self-contained lives. Phil Baines found that when he had a burglary this broke the ice and enabled him to have a real conversation with his neighbours for the first time.

Holy Trinity, Nailsea, are thinking of planting another church in an estate near the parish church, which is virgin territory as far as the church is concerned. They are looking at the possibility prayerfully, and asking the church membership to pray about it. They need some green lights before they go ahead: a suitable venue, a lay-led team to staff it, and finance. It will not be an easy task, and they need to carry the rest of the church with them. There are many such new estates up and down the country which have not been touched for the Kingdom of God. But the experience of both St Mary's, Stoke-sub-Hamdon and Holy Trinity, Nailsea is that when the original novelty has worn off, the new churches will need perseverance and discipline to carry the mission through.

I cannot imagine that the rebuilding of the walls of faith throughout the country will be any different. Now, I believe, is God's time, *kairos*, for this to happen. The fields are ready for harvesting, but it is not until we have experienced spiritual renewal and revival as a Church that we will have the strength not just to do the work, but to persevere until we are able to celebrate together, because the walls of faith have been rebuilt.

Four times in the last chapter of his book, Nehemiah asks to be remembered by God for what he has done for Israel. By being made part of the Canon of the Old Testament, he has been remembered, not just by God but by succeeding generations. For this generation, however, I believe he has a special message, because for us, as for him, the time has come to rebuild.

A Prayer of Sir Francis Drake

Which he made before the battle against
the Spanish Armada.

O Lord God, when thou givest to thy servants to endeavour any great matter, grant us also to know that it is not the beginning, but the continuing of the same unto the end, until it be thoroughly finished, which yieldeth the true glory; through him who for the finishing of thy work laid down his life, our Redeemer, Jesus Christ. Amen.

Study

BIBLE READING: NEHEMIAH 13

QUESTIONS FOR MEDITATION/DISCUSSION

1. What does chapter 13 have to tell us about Nehemiah as a leader?
2. What does chapter 13 have to tell us about discipline and perseverance?
3. What discipline and perseverance does the Church need if it is to rebuild the walls of faith?

PRAYER

Pray through the issues raised by the questions, ending with Sir Francis Drake's prayer.